To John & Sue.
Best wishes
Mark

FROM DRAGON TO DRAGON

FROM DRAGON TO DRAGON

Mark Isaac-Williams

The Book Guild Ltd
Sussex, England

First published in Great Britain in 2004 by
The Book Guild Ltd,
25 High Street,
Lewes, East Sussex
BN7 2LU

Typesetting in Times by
IML Typographers, Birkenhead, Merseyside

Printed in Great Britain by
CPI Bath

A catalogue record for this book is
available from The British Library

ISBN 1 85776 877 9

This book is dedicated to my parents and their many friends who encouraged me to record this part of their lives.

‘The Dragon was the rain spirit of the ancient Chinese. Unlike the Western monster, the Chinese ‘*loong*’ was not an evil creature malevolent to mankind, but the rain giver who gathered the clouds, brought the welcome moisture and presided over water.’

ACKNOWLEDGEMENTS

My grateful thanks to Barbara Anslow of Frinton-on-Sea, Essex, who was the hospital secretary in Stanley Internment Camp, Hong Kong, during the war and who painstakingly read through my original manuscript.

Thanks too, to Hugh Roberts, of Halstead, Essex whom I had met many years ago in Hong Kong and who, after hearing that I was writing this story, kindly offered me some photographs of Hong Kong and Japanese Prisoners of War that he had taken in 1945 while serving in the Navy.

And to all my friends who continued to encourage me to keep on to the end – thanks.

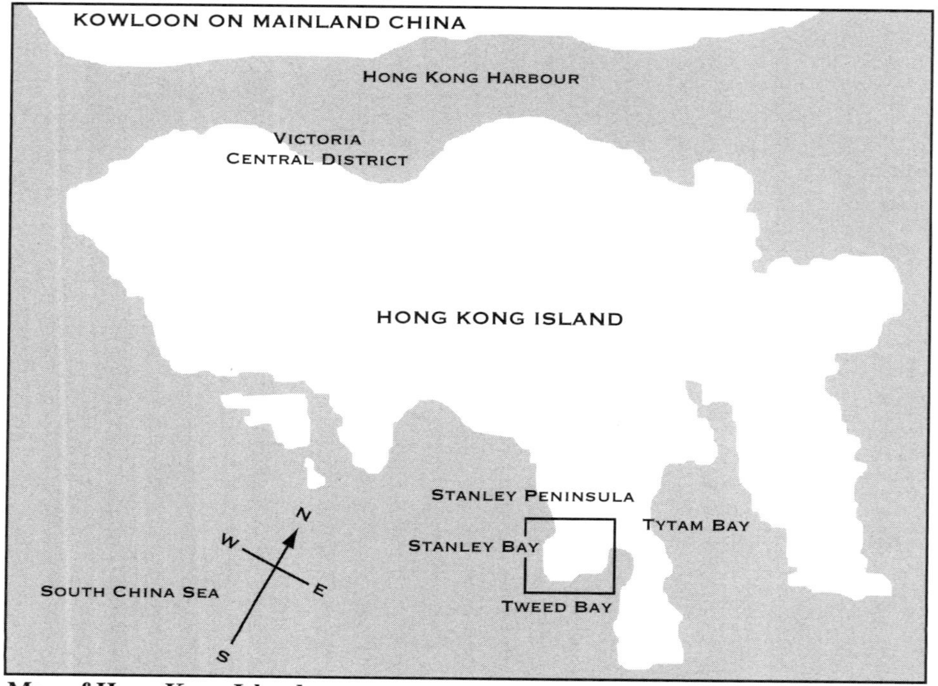

Map of Hong Kong Island

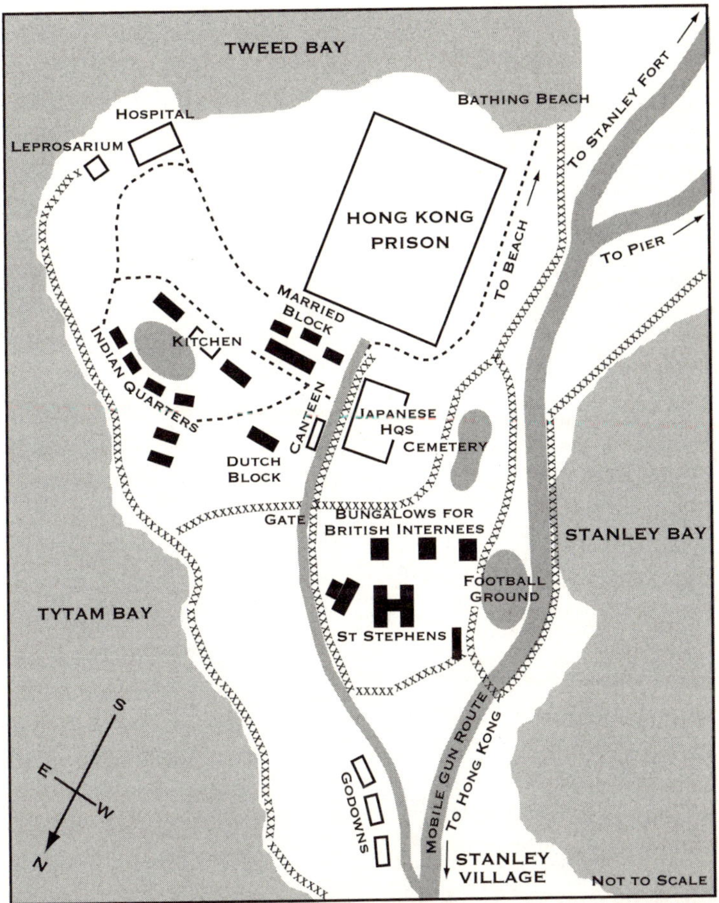

Hong Kong - Internment Camp on Stanley Peninsula 1941-1945

■	Living blocks	xxx	Barbed wire
▒	Main road	---	Footpath

As Margery put down the phone she turned to her colleagues and said, 'Guess what? I am going to China to be married.'

The year was 1935 and my mother was working in the National Provincial Bank in Newport, Monmouth, where most of the population had never left Wales, let alone travelled to the opposite side of the world.

In the West, people knew China as a place of intrigue and excitement, of secret societies and opium, and men with long pigtails; a place of danger and intrigue and one where heroin was included in the price of an hotel room. It was another world.

THE GATEWAY TO CHINA

Shanghai, where mother was bound, was China's premier financial and commercial centre and the fourth largest port in the world. There was no other city in the Far East that could begin to compare with this treaty port. It was the most corrupt, vice-ridden and decadent place imaginable. It commanded access to the Yangtze, which was navigable for 2,000 miles and the principal means of communication. Rising in the Kun Lun Mountains north of Tibet and flowing through Wuhan and Nanking (the old capital), the Yangtze finally reaches the sea via its last tributary, the Huangpo, and the port of Shanghai. It was originally built on mudflats which were only just above sea level, hence the name *Shang hai* which in Chinese is written as two characters, meaning 'above sea level'.

Most of the city sprawled behind the Bund, which was the heart of this ugly, and yet in many ways, attractive city. At the southernmost end, ships unloaded their cargo and coolies could be seen straining under enormous loads as they moved the goods to the godowns. At the junction of Avenue Edouard VII and the Bund was the boundary between the International Settlement, which housed the British, and the French Concession, which housed French compatriots. The Bund (waterfront street), curving along the banks of the Huangpo River, was Shanghai's main artery and accommodated some of the tallest buildings in Asia. Here could be seen the imposing Corinthian-columned front of the Hong Kong and Shanghai Bank guarded by two enormous crouching bronze lions one each side of the front door, a symbol of prosperity and might; the Cathay Hotel (now the Peace Hotel) with its marble pillars and staircase, mahogany reception desk and Art Deco, where my parents were to hold their wedding reception. To the left of the Hong Kong and Shanghai Bank was, and still is, the Shanghai Customs House, recognised by its large-faced clock and from where the Chinese Maritime Customs Service was administered. Occupying No. 1 on the Bund was the Shanghai Club, noted for the longest bar in the world and originally built as an exclusive men's club. A place where all Shanghai's foreign leading citizens regularly called in the evening to knock back a gin and bitters before dining upstairs.

With a population of nearly 4 million, Shanghai was classed with Tokyo, Berlin, Moscow, London and New York and was known as 'The Gateway to China' or, and less appreciated by the Chinese, 'The Paris of the Orient'. It was in the early 1930s that Shanghai, more than any other city in China, had its greatest allure to foreigners heading to the Far East. It was large, it was rich and it was heading towards its peak of prosperity. Foreign investors had poured in more than 3 billion dollars – at the time, the largest outside investment in any world city.

It was a place of riotous abundance for the 48,000 foreigners and the rich Chinese alike, with no limit to what could be achieved and bought. Whilst the rest of the world was experiencing the Great Depression of the '30s, the city barely knew it existed – this was Shanghai's finest hour.

History

In 1863, Shanghai was divided into two foreign settlements, i.e. the International Settlement, made up of mainly the British and some Americans, and the French Concession. (Later the Japanese acquired extra territorial and commercial rights within this settlement, but it remained British dominated and ruled by the Municipal Council until the war). Within those few miles Shanghai seemed less like the commercial centre of China than an extension of a vast universal metropolis. By 1930 the port of Shanghai had increased and so too had the foreign settlements. Together, the two areas accounted for 12 square miles, whilst the Chinese sector was only 8 square miles. These sectors had no obvious dividing line, but in spite of this, the two foreign settlements always felt safe. The areas were fronted by the Huangpo River, where warships and gunboats of European powers were always anchored, together with luxury cruise liners, rusty old tramp steamers and Chinese junks. Forty-eight different nationalities existed in Shanghai in the 1930s, including white Russian refugees who had fled from the Bolsheviks, some very influential Iraqi Jews, and a police force of Sikhs recruited from India. It was a free city and open to all, with nearly a dozen foreign newspapers – four English, one French, one Russian, one German and one American. The currency, strange as it may seem, was the Mexican dollar brought in via the Philippines as a left-over legacy of the Spanish trade there.

Shanghai was not just a port but a major industrial centre.

The Japanese were first to set up industrial plants to exploit cheap labour, soon followed by other foreign countries. Factories belched out black smoke causing unbearable pollution and at times the only respite was the sea breeze along the Bund. It was of no consequence to the busy, money-making people of the city.

China at that time was ruled by the Kuomintang (Nationalist) Government led by Generalissimo Chiang Kai-shek, and the Japanese, who already had a foothold in the north, were just waiting for a chance to launch a full-scale invasion of the country. The Nationalist Government claimed to control nearly half the population of China, but in fact its political authority was very weak, although this was not immediately apparent. At the beginning of the war it had enjoyed a wave of national and international support.

MY PARENTS

Born Eleanor Margery Isaac on 30th September 1908 in the small market town of Brecon, South Wales, my mother was the youngest of eight children in a very happy, middle-class farming family, with a Welsh father and an English mother from Stratford-on-Avon. Castle Farm, which was opposite St David's Chuch, was situated on the Llanfais road (Newgate Road) surrounded by acres of farm land. Today, due to the building of more homes etc., the land no longer exists but up until a few years ago the almost original farm house was used as an hotel named the Castle Farm Hotel. Her baby years were spent with older brothers and sisters who pushed her to the top of the Brecon Beacons in a pram. They were a fun-loving, mischievous bunch of youngsters enjoying life to the full. By the time she was 20, both parents were dead and so were some of her siblings. Her closest sister Muriel died of a ruptured appendix when she was only 15 and her middle brother Cyril, who falsified his age (he was only 17) in order to sign up for the army, was killed in the 1914–18 war at Ypres. Those who remained had left Brecon to either pursue their careers or study. Margery spent the weekends in Abergavenny with friends who played tennis regularly, but she had lodgings in Newport during the week when she worked in the bank. It was on one of those numerous train journeys back to Newport that she met my father.

At the time, Leonard Hinckley Williams was studying for his Master's Certificate in Cardiff and he too travelled every weekend between Cardiff and Hereford. While waiting for a train one weekend he heard Margery tell someone that she was from Brecon. Since his family was also from Brecon he struck up a conversation with her and discovered they had friends and family in common. For the following weeks he kept an eye open for her at the station and whenever he had any time off, would visit her in Newport.

My father's passion was the sea and he had joined his first ship as an apprentice in the Trinity House service at the age of 15. Many years and examinations later, during the great depression of the '30s, work was difficult to find, even for a seafarer, and Leonard found jobs far and few between. He was born in Cape Town, South Africa, on 12th December 1906, where his parents had married on 14th September 1904. Why my grandparents were married in the Cape instead of Brecon, where the family home was, will always remain somewhat of a mystery.

From the Cape, my grandparents eventually returned to the UK, where my father's brother Hyatt and his sister Gwenda were born. After completing their schooling in an UK boarding school, the family finally left for Australia, except my father, who remained behind to start his career as a mariner.

Leonard completed his final Master's Certificate examinations in 1934, passing with top marks. There were few jobs in sight, but he managed to find work as a second mate in Southern Railway Steamers out of Southampton. This was followed by a short stint as master of a cargo ship running from Cardiff to Buenos Aires, South America, and after several more months of temporary work Leonard was offered the choice of delivering a ship to Shanghai with an option to join the Chinese Maritime Customs on arrival, or delivering the ship and then returning to Britain. He discussed this with Margery and they decided that he should stay in Shanghai with certain employment, rather than return to uncertainty in the UK. It was then that he proposed to my mother – it was 1st April 1935 and he wasn't fooling when he asked her to get married in Shanghai.

SLOW BOAT TO CHINA

The SS *Ullesmere* had been bought for £16,000 by the Chinese Maritime Customs and Leonard was summoned to Sunderland to meet the captain and an all-Chinese crew who had been rounded up as dead-beats in Antwerp. As he boarded he noticed an ensign that was quite unknown to him, and was informed that it was the naval ensign of the Chinese Kuomintang Government.

En route to Shanghai the ship was to load coal in Durban for discharge in Colombo, but it was not long before Leonard discovered that the ship had been laid up for five years and was not exactly in a very seaworthy condition. In fact, the master of the tug remarked that he would be surprised if they ever made it to Shanghai! 'Good luck,' he said.

The journey was a saga of catastrophies – bilges filled with coal, hatches filled with water and crew trying to murder each other. It was a mate's nightmare. By late December the ship had reached the southern end of Formosa (Taiwan), and whilst they were steaming along the

Pescadores Channel they were approached by an aggressive Japanese light cruiser training her main guns on the *Ullesmere* (possibly because she was flying the Chinese naval ensign). It was a tense moment but the cruiser eventually moved away without incident.

On arrival in Shanghai the ship had to be extensively fitted out and repaired and she was finally commissioned in early 1937 as CPS (Customs Preventive Ship) *Fuhsing*. She only managed a couple of patrols for the Chinese Customs before being captured by the Japanese in November 1937 in Shanghai.

In early 1936 Leonard signed a three-year contract with the Chinese Maritime Customs, in which he was to honourably serve for 14 years until 12th December 1949. Perhaps it would have been longer had it not been for the civil war in China resulting in the downfall of the Kuomintang and consequently the Chinese Maritime Customs.

At that time, very little was known in the West about this service, and even today few people have heard it.

THE IMPERIAL CHINESE MARITIME CUSTOMS SERVICE

The Treaty of Nanking, signed in 1842, did away with the single port to which foreigners could trade, i.e. Canton. The previous year, Hong Kong, which was made up of the Island of Victoria and the tip of the Kowloon Peninsula, had been ceded to Britain and five treaty ports were opened to foreign trade. China and Britain agreed that consuls should be appointed to reside in these ports to ensure that the merchant trade paid all just dues. By 1854 the collection of revenue, due to changes in government, had almost disappeared and the consuls, in order to comply with the terms of the various treaties, decided to collect the revenue from their own nationals with a view to handing it over to China, if and when a stable government was established. When this did take place, the Chinese were so surprised that they suggested the formation of a service staffed by foreigners and answerable to Peking, and later, a local manned service to collect the revenue. Such was the inception of the Imperial Chinese Maritime Customs Service, and as more treaty ports were opened up, it became necessary to establish a fleet of revenue cruisers and launches to steer foreign trade through the correct channels.

Since the object was to ensure that all cargo from overseas passed through the treaty ports, Chinese flag vessels could be boarded on the high seas, and this was usually done within a 3-mile limit off the coastal territorial waters, although China actually claimed a 12½-half mile radius.

The Customs Service was unique in many ways and had no parallel anywhere in the world. It began very modestly in 1864 during the Ch'ing Dynasty and the Taiping Rebellion and eventually became the foremost revenue collector in China, and the mainstay of organising trade between China and the rest of the world. It was to be responsible for arranging for China to participate in no fewer than 28 international exhibitions from the Paris Exhibition of 1867 to the one at Liège in 1905.

Unlike other customs services around the world, China's service did not confine its work to ordinary customs routine. At the time when there were no diplomatic or consular agents in China, the Customs Service, which was a Chinese institution with a staff of picked men from the leading nations, became a trusted counsellor and guide to both the provincial authorities and the Peking Government. Later, with the growth of a Diplomatic Service and the development of higher education based on Western lines, that function fell into abeyance. But it was the support the

Customs Service gave to the T'ung Wen Kuan (the Old College of Peking) that enabled China to train her first diplomats and so lay the foundation for the Consular and Diplomatic Services.

Once the Government had finally disposed of the Taiping insurgents, with advice from the Customs Service, it was able to erect the most modern lighthouses and aids to navigation along the coast and waterways of China. Up until the Japanese War in 1941, the China coast was recognised as one of the best marked in the world, while the sunken rocks, channels and shifting shoals in the Yangtze were marked by lightships, buoys and beacons regularly tended by the Customs Marine Department. This department also carried out all surveys of coast, harbours and rivers for the Government before the Hydrographic Bureau was formed, and published numerous charts which were still in use in the 1930s.

One of the Customs Service's tasks was to supervise measures for the prevention of disease from ship-borne infection. Everything connected with foreign trade, shipping and domestic trade carried in foreign-style vessels, was automatically referred to the Customs, who would take necessary action according to circumstances. Later, the National Quarantine Bureau came into existence and the Customs was released from that role.

Local interests also demanded the attention of the Customs Service which, with the Government's sanction, collected consolidated tax at specified ports. For example, there were the 'dike' dues at Ichang, Shasi, Hankow, Yochow and Changsha; 'breakwater' dues at Chefoo; 'river' dues, bridge tax and the Halho Improvement surtax at Tientsin; 'bund' dues at Amoy; 'mule' tax at Tengyueh and 'wharfage' and 'conservancy' dues at other ports.

Another duty the Customs Service performed was the publication of trade statistics and trade reports. To begin with, the annual returns and reports were printed locally at each port, but during the 1860s the work was centred at the Customs House in Shanghai and in 1873 at the Statistical Department which was especially formed for the purpose. It was an enormous undertaking.

Besides the voluminous annual trade reports and inspectorate instructions in the form of circulars and memoranda, the department issued a series of detailed reports on lights, buoys and beacons; a special series of medical reports; a collection of China's treaties with foreign states and hundreds of monographs dealing with such items as opium, silk, medicines, tea, Chinese music, jute, furs, skins, ginseng, hospitals, collection or disposal of revenue, timber rafts on the Yangtze etc. etc. Later on, with its up-to-date printing machine, electrically controlled tabulating machine and work which was technically excellent, the Statistical Department was to become the envy of many a government around the world.

Finally, the last duty undertaken by the Customs Service was the administration of the postal service, later to become the National Post Office of China in 1896 under the direction of the Inspector General of Customs and Post. By 1911 the Postal Service was financially independent enough to pass from the control of the Customs to become a department of the Yu-ch'uan Pu (Board of Posts and Communications).

By 1898 large parts of Chinese territory had been conceded to the Germans, with a Custom House being set up in Tsingtao (1899) after the cession of Kiachow on lease to Germany. The area was to be temporarily ruled as German and was treated as a special area into which foreign and Chinese goods could be imported free, only to become dutiable if re-exported into Chinese territory. Moreover, the Commissioner of the Chinese Customs at Tsingtao was to be of German nationality and so too the European staff, with all correspondence between the Customs office and German merchants and authorities being in the German language. This was very quickly proved impractical because the German authorities were unwilling to allow the Chinese Customs to actually function in the leased German territory. Hart (the Commissioner) insisted on forming a chain of customs stations on the Chinese side to keep a check on all goods entering and leaving, but further negotiations led to an agreement by the German Government with the Chinese Customs to help safeguard the revenue in the leased territory for 20 per cent of import duty on goods in return.

Appointment of Commissioner Hart

In 1859 Robert Hart, who had come straight from Queen's University, Belfast, to China, was appointed Deputy Commissioner of the Custom House. He had resigned from the British Consular Service for this purpose and was eventually to become the Inspector General (Commissioner) at 28 years of age in November 1863. It was an appointment which would take Hart through a career of 50 years in the Chinese Customs Service, a career unparalleled in the annals of the Far East, during which time he was able to do more for his adopted land than any other foreigner before or since.

Hart was a fluent mandarin (the language of Court officials and North China) speaker and, combined with his tact, modesty, soundness of advice, sanity of judgement and thorough knowledge of the treaties and their bearing on Customs work, was able to win the complete confidence and respect of Chinese high officials. He had the ear of the Empress Dowager T'zu-hsi and her advisor Prince Kung, so much so that the Prince ordered Hart to take up permanent residence in Peking so that he could call on him at any time. Prince Kung relied totally on Hart who was well-versed in foreign ways and whose advice he completely trusted. He was to become one of the most powerful foreigners in China.

In 1869, Hart reorganised some of the main service. He made provisions for a foreign indoor staff of 17 commissioners, 6 deputy commissioners and 90 assistants, while the Chinese staff would have 70 linguists in various grades as well as writers and teachers. The outdoor staff was to include 30 tide surveyors, 30 examiners and 160 tidewaiters (all foreigners), with a number of Chinese employees working as boatmen and messengers.

In addition to a salary, crew could also earn seizure money. This was based on the ultimate value of the seizure and varied from 30 per cent of the value if armed combat had taken place, to 20 per cent for a seizure made as the result of a normal search and 10 per cent when the seizure was made as a result of information. Chefoo in North China was considered to be one of the best ports, since vessels based there were in a position to intercept smugglers from Manchuria. The port of Foochow covered the route from Formosa and Swatow; Kowloon covered the smugglers from Hong Kong, and Hoi How on Hainan Island covered Indo-China and Kwanchowan, which was then a French colony.

Hart's aim was to give each country trading with China a rough proportionate representation of indoor staff, which became more difficult as the Service grew. In 1873 when the first service list was compiled there was an indoor staff of 95 – British, French, German, American, Norwegian, Russian and Swiss. In 1911 there was a total staff of 1,345 foreigners (British, German, Japanese, French, Swedish, Spanish, Korean, American, Russian, Italian, Portuguese, Norwegian, Danish, Belgian and Dutch) and 5,885 Chinese. Because it was so cosmopolitan, staff developed a unique camaraderie, possibly unparalleled anywhere else in the world, and this did much to stabilise and render the service of great utility to China – more so than if the staff had only been drawn from the great powers of the time.

All foreign Customs officials had the right to punish

offences against the revenue by either confiscation or fine. This was often questioned by the consuls and fiercely contested by foreign merchants.

After several years of experiment and negotiations, Hart eventually set out his *8 Rules for Joint Investigation in cases of Fine and Confiscation by the Custom House Authorities*, which were issued to all the ports in 1868. The rules were seldom used but they did serve as a preventative influence for over 60 years until 1932, when they were superseded.

In 1882 Hart was created KCMG and was offered the post of British Minister and Plenipotentiary in Peking by the British Minister, Lord Granville, on the death of Sir Harry Parkes. Hart arranged for his brother James Hart to succeed him as Commissioner of Customs, but there were other candidates equally suited to the post and likely to cause international rivalry. At the request of the Dowager Empress and to the relief of the Customs, Hart decided to remain in the post as Commissioner – a post he had made so famous and one which he was better qualified to fill than anyone else.

He would remain there until he was 73 years of age,when he finally left the country to which he had given so much of his life, to live in England. He had seen China awaken from her ancient state of seclusion to a modern state of internationalism and with the sound guidance he was always ready to impart, had the satisfaction of seeing the Customs Service recognised, not only as a sign and symbol of the Central Government's authority, but more importantly as a unifying agency. He had inspired the men of this service with loyalty to China and was showered with rare honours by the Chinese: the Order of the Red Button of the First Class; Ancestral Rank of the First Class for Three Generations; the Peacock's Feather; the First Class of the Second Division of the Order of the Double Dragon and, most coveted of all, the title of 'Senior Guardian of the Heir Apparent'. He was given no fewer than 11 grand crosses from other countries and a GCMG and Baronetcy by Great Britain. Sir Robert passed away on 20th September 1911 in Marlow, Buckinghamshire.

Such was the background to the service my father joined on 19th January 1936 when there were about 950 foreign staff and about 8,500 Chinese. He signed a contract for three years, after which he would have been given a passage back to the United Kingdom with six months' paid leave. In spite of having a Master's Foreign-going Certificate, he was appointed Second Officer (on probation) at $280 (£17 10s) per month.

One of his first trips was to North China, where for several months of the year the Gulf of Peichile is frozen solid. In Chefoo Harbour, where some of the vessels were based, he often went ashore in a rickshaw; from the ship's side across the ice to the shore, the coolie would run with great agility and care. When Leonard arrived, the ice had only just begun to break up but it was sufficient to allow them to tend the North East Promontory Light Station. It had been a 'seven coat' winter. In conditions such as these, the Chinese sew themselves into as many padded coats as they can until they are eventually wearing seven or even more if the winter is exceptionally cold. At the beginning of spring and warmer weather, the locals could be seen by the roadside removing coat by coat and de-lousing themselves. The odour was not to be sniffed at!

On 9th September 1936, my mother set sail from Southampton to Shanghai on a Japanese ship, the *Yasakuri Maru*. With her three-tiered wedding cake, made by family friends in Brecon, and her wedding dress from Harrods, she boarded with excitement and intrepidity. On board was the Japanese Olympic team returning to Japan after the 1936

Berlin Olympics. Before reaching Shanghai, Margery noticed that the team was throwing flower wreaths overboard. One of the members told her that it was in honour of a former tennis player who had committed suicide by jumping overboard. Having lost at Wimbledon, he could not face returning to his motherland. Margery was a keen and competitive sportswoman and she thought this a rather drastic step to take for losing a game. It was incomprehensible, but it made her realise for the first time just how very different Japanese culture was.

On the ship my mother first experienced chopsticks. Wearing full evening dress (as was customary for dinner in those days) and sitting on deck with some of the Japanese sportsmen, she proceeded to drop most of the rice down the front of her dress. This produced a lot of tittering behind hands from the Japanese women but, undeterred, she struggled on and soon became very adept.

The voyage took exactly one month and mother arrived in Shanghai on 9th October 1936. Leaning on the ship's railings as the *Yasakuri Maru* wound her way up the Huangpo, passing warehouses, shipyards, grimy docks, cotton mills and lumber yards, she noticed naval warships, American merchant vessels and P & O mail steamers intermingled with a variety of typical Chinese craft, sampans and junks, and fishing boats with painted eyes on their bows (to ward off evil) and enormous rattan sails. Everywhere she looked there was movement and activity. Finally as the ship made a sharp turn left, Margery was totally unprepared for the sight that presented itself. With its imposing marble and granite buildings, fronted by a long boulevard and grassy promenade, the Bund looked more like a city in Europe than China. It was not what she had expected.

Leonard was waiting on the wharf as the ship berthed and after organising the delivery of Margery's trunks, took her ashore.

Driving in a taxi along the length of the Bund, the noise was cacophonous. As every conceivable mode of transport – buses, rickshaws, hand carts, horse carts, bicycles, motor bikes and wheelbarrows – jostled for a space, so too could every conceivable noise be heard as street vendors shouted, horns honked, bells rang, whistles blew, blind men banged their gongs, and rickshaw coolies barked their way through a continuous stream of pedestrians arduously trying to cross. This normal yet disorderly everyday life of Shanghai was both disturbing and fascinating to Margery.

The following day my parents were married in the Holy Trinity Cathedral, Nanking Road. It was 10th October, known as the 'Double Tenth', the Anniversary of the Foundation of the Republic of China, and was a public holiday – the only day that Leonard could arrange the wedding as he had not been granted leave at any other time. My mother knew no one at her wedding, not even her matron-of-honour. The reception was held at the Cathay Hotel, where they were to stay until a furnished flat became available in the Bubbling Well Road a few weeks later.

Following his wedding day, Leonard returned to work, which often took him away for long periods at a time. Fortunately Margery's matron-of -honour was a keen hockey player and persuaded her to start playing again. She then played on a regular basis at the Race Club, eventually representing the Shanghai team as centre forward in the Interport against Hong Kong in 1937 (a few years later she represented Hong Kong against Shanghai). The ladies' team, together with a men's football team, travelled to Hong Kong by ship for the game – it ended in a draw.

Margery was also a good tennis player, having played regularly in the UK, so this too helped to keep her busy while Leonard was often away at sea, and through her sporting activities she made many friends. But she was not aware, and soon discovered, that this international city, unlike other cosmopolitan cities in the world, had a stuffy downside.

The different nationalities, British, American, French, German, etc., rarely mixed. The British lived their British way of life: cricket, lawn bowls, sailing regattas and an ultra-snobbish country club. Americans had their own community with their own school and club, so too the Russians, French and Italians. The parties were also completely British or American, Russian or French etc., until slowly things began to change and there were parties that included Chinese bankers, diplomats and rich young business men with their wives and concubines.

That first Christmas after they were married the houseboy said, 'Missy, you likee big bird for Christmas? I go catchee one.' Margery gathered that he meant a turkey and said she would leave it to him to arrange. On 23rd December she heard a commotion outside their flat and on opening the door found the houseboy leading the turkey upstairs on a string. She did not realise that in China birds of any type, pigeons, ducks, chickens, turkeys etc., are all bought alive and prepared just before being cooked. Not quite what my mother had expected!

Meanwhile Leonard was enjoying his work and was delighted when he was very quickly promoted to Acting First Officer. His contract was cancelled and he was put on the permanent staff and appointed to CLT (Customs Light Tender) *Haihsing* the light tender in which he had previously served.

THE 'SOONG DYNASTY'

The Soong sisters and their brother were four of six children born to an American-missionary-educated Chinese, Sung Chiao-shun (later named Charlie Soong), and Ni Kweitseng, also a missionary-educated Methodist from one of Shanghai's oldest Christian gentry families.

Ai-ling, the eldest girl, Ching-ling and Mei-ling all attended the posh McTyeire School in Shanghai and later, on the insistence of their father, were the first Chinese women to be enrolled at the Wesleyan College for Women in Georgia, USA.

Their brother, T.V. Soong, went to Harvard to study finance and eventually, through his control of the Central Bank of China, was rumoured at one time to be the world's richest man. These four were the basis of the 'Soong Dynasty'. Ai-ling married H.H. Kung, who had a large fortune and an obsession for making money. He knew very little about modern banking and on occasions when he alternated with his brother-in-law, T.V. Soong as Finance Minister, caused complete chaos.

Second daughter Ching-ling, being an idealist rather than a romantic, wanted to help save China and having once been his English language secretary, renewed her friendship with Dr Sun Yat-sen (Founder of the Republic of China). Against her father's orders, she ran away to Tokyo and married Sun.

It was Ai-ling who conceived and arranged the grand alliance between third sister Mei-ling and the future leader of China, Chiang Kai-shek.

Mei-ling was pampered, yet clever, with a degree in English literature. In great demand as a guest at dinner parties in the best of Shanghai circles, Mei-ling attended gala race meetings, planned fashion shows, played tennis and organised Church and YWCA functions. She craved luxury and money and in later life, as Madame Chiang Kai-shek, was noted for her extravagances; 'numerous fur coats, toeless shoes, designer handbags and diamond earrings' all betrayed her 'expensive state of mind', (according to journalist John Gunther.)

CIVIL WAR

During the period 1930 to late 1936 China had been in a constant state of civil war between the Communists and the Nationalists (Kuomintang), and Generalissimo Chiang Kai-shek (leader of the KMT) continually launched campaigns to eliminate the Communist threat. Not always successful, Chiang decided in 1931 to lead the campaign himself, and as he was moving towards the Communist capital of Juichin he received news of the Mukden incident, and this caused him to abandon his campaign. Cleverly, in absorbing Manchuria, the Japanese pretended that the Chinese were plotting to destroy the railway between Mukden and Port Arthur (so fiercely fought for by the Russians and Japanese and lost by the Russians in 1905). They used this deceit to justify their seizure of arsenals in Mukden and other Manchurian towns, and by the time Chiang's army withdrew, Manchuria was firmly in Japanese hands. In one short stroke the Chinese Maritime Customs was excluded from all the Manchurian ports, causing a major blow to their revenue, and as the Japanese gradually extended their territorial control towards Peking, the Customs mobility was severely affected. In January 1932 the Japanese attacked the KMT positions around Shanghai, which further weakened Chinese control of the city. It was not good news for the Inspectorate, which was now located there.

That summer the Kuomintang again launched more attacks against the Communists, often with heavy losses. When, in December 1936, Chiang flew to Sian (Xian) to urge for a greater effort by his troops, he was told that the troops would rather be fighting the Japanese than their own fellow countrymen. There followed a series of unexplained negotiations between Chiang Kai-shek and Chou En-lai (the Communist representative) which resulted in the 1936 agreement and Chiang being arrested and then freed (as long as he agreed to end the campaigns against the Communists and join forces for the good of China).

The Japanese had already made great advances into China between 1934 and 1937, having reached Inner Mongolia and the northern part of Hopei.

On 7th July 1937, while Leonard was out on a mission, another Japanese-fabricated incident broke out in Lukou-chiao near the Marco Polo Bridge south of Peking. The Japanese claimed that whilst their troops were performing night manoeuvres, Chinese troops fired on them – it was just the excuse they needed for a full-scale war. The invasion was rapid, and in North China Japanese troops advanced along main railway lines and the Chinese forces fell back. Peking and Tientsin fell on 28th and 29th July respectively and this paved the way for their advance through Chahar and part of Suiyuan to reach the upper Yellow River at Paotow to the west, and to the south along the rail lines to Hankow, Nanking and Sian.

On 8th August 1937 the Japanese launched an amphibious invasion on Shanghai, which was met with more resistance than they had ever imagined. Chiang Kai-shek had chosen his best divisions to protect the city and as the Chinese held on, the second battle for Shanghai was, for a time, in the balance, until the Japanese were able to get reinforcements.

On 14th August 1937, bombs began to explode in two of Shanghai's busiest intersections – one fell on the Palace Hotel in the International Settlement on the corner of Nanjing Road and the Bund, one just missed the Cathay Hotel opposite, and another in Frenchtown at Avenue Edouard VII. On Bloody Saturday, as it was later to be remembered, nearly 1,600 Chinese and some foreigners died before they knew what had hit them, with around 1,400 wounded. No one could have foretold the catastrophe that was to happen that hot Saturday afternoon. Within moments of Nanjing Road being ripped apart, 700 people lay dead, many with heads, arms and legs severed from their bodies. It was not the Japanese who had caused the mayhem but the Chinese themselves.

That morning, Chinese bombers had tried to sink the Japanese flagship cruiser *Idzumo* without success. In the late afternoon, making a second attempt, five twin-engined Chinese bombers appeared out of nowhere heading for *Idzumo* anchored at the north end of the Huangpo River. The bombers ran head on into a barrage of Japanese anti-aircraft fire. Panicking, one bomber peeled off in a dive, jettisoning four bombs as he went, one of which went through the roof of the Palace Hotel, another landed in front of the Cathay Hotel next door and two others veered and were caught by the wind, sending them hurtling towards the crowded Bund. Half an hour later, after it appeared to be over, the silence was once more interrupted – another stricken bomber had accidentally released two more bombs at the intersection of Avenue Edouard VII and Tibet Road. The busiest square in Frenchtown was demolished and so too were another thousand or so Chinese and foreigners. It was one of the worst single-day civilian carnages of the time.

Meanwhile, the British had endeavoured to negotiate with the Japanese, but by now there was no chance of a truce. In spite of this, the battle for Shanghai continued over three months until the Japanese troops landed on the coast south of the city. Many of the Chinese troops fled into the French Concession rather than surrender to the Japanese. Refugees poured in for protection but the International Settlement was no longer part of an empire and the Japanese demanded more power to administer what remained. It was the beginning of the end for Shanghai, which finally fell to the Japanese on 8 November 1937. The Foreign Settlement became no man's land and crime and terror took over. Shanghai declined so fast that it lost the trade of the Yangtze Basin, which had made it the great trading city that it was.

*   *   *

My father returned to port at the end of July and on 8th August was told to report to his ship immediately. As he left Margery he said, 'I think we may be going to Kuikiang and I will be back in about ten days.' Little did he know that it would be nearly 13 months before he would see her again.

Towards the end of October that year, Radio Tokyo announced in English that the Ministry of Finance and H.H. Kung (married to one of the three Soong sisters, Ai-ling, and Chiang Kai-shek's brother-in-law) were leaving Nanking. At 10 p.m. that night, someone from the Ministry boarded father's ship with top secret information that the family of the Minister of Finance and certain foreign advisors would be embarking at 2 a.m. for passage to Hankow and that they were to pick up the Minister off Wuhu the following morning. The foreign advisors were a representative of the Skoda Arms Works (Czechoslovakian) and two Americans, Layton and Pauley, who were interested in the Vultec Aviation Corporation, which was building fighter aircraft for China.

That afternoon H.H. Kung embarked to join his wife and two daughters, who were already on board, and the plan was to meet a seaplane off Anking the following afternoon and transfer them to a flight for Hankow. The following day there was driving rain, gale force winds and huge swells as a result of a strong north east monsoon, so common at that time of the year. The ship eventually reached Anking but there was no sign of the seaplane. An hour later the noise of an aircraft was heard up-river and they were relieved to see a small seaplane overhead. The pilot, who was a foreigner, indicated that he would alight further up-river where the water was a little calmer.

Having anchored off the creek, Leonard went over to the landed aircraft in a launch and was informed that all was ready and that His Excellency could embark.

Due to rough water it was not possible to rig the accommodation ladder over the ship's side, so the only way His Excellency could reach the launch was down the pilot ladder hanging over the side of the ship. Not only did he decline to do this, but having looked over the side, was promptly sick!

After a long delay all foreign passengers were transferred to the seaplane and the ship sailed on to Hankow, where she arrived the following day without incident and berthed alongside the pontoon to which HMS *Cape Town* was moored. Armed guards were stationed on the pontoon and along the side of the ship, causing great interest to the crew of HMS *Cape Town*. Having then dismissed the guards, my father was surprised to see Layton and Pauley (the two Americans) returning on board with a bottle of gin in each hand. Knowing that the ship's rations had been cut off for quite a long period, they thought that this would be a very welcome gift.

In early December 1937 one forenoon, Leonard's commander returned on board from his usual visit to the Hankow Commissioner to inform his crew that at sunset that day, they would be decommissioned in order to become a German merchant vessel.

The following day at 8 a.m., the German Ambassador to China and the Chinese Minister of Foreign Affairs, Dr Wellington Koo, embarked for their voyage to Nanking. Generalissimo Chiang Kai-shek and his wife were also to have boarded but changed their minds at the last moment and flew by seaplane instead. The German Ambassador's mission was to act as an intermediary between the Chinese and the Japanese with a view to bringing an end to the so-called Sino-Japanese incident. The Japanese had by now complete control of China's North East Provinces – the whole of the rail line from Peking to Nanking was in their hands and the eastern corridor from Shanghai to the north was under their occupation, as well as their warships patrolling the South China coast to prevent military supplies reaching the Nationalist Government. They offered Chiang Kai-shek peace terms which were refused because they required him to recognise the puppet state of Manchukuo which had been established in Manchuria under the last Emperor, Pu-yi, on 18th February 1932.

The conference turned out to be fruitless and a complete waste of time, and Leonard's ship returned to Hankow the following day. Unable to force Chiang Kai-shek to surrender, Japan's alternative solution was to set up puppet regimes in parts of China which were already under Japanese control.

Nanking, situated on the Chang Jiang River and north west of Shanghai, was the capital of China at the time and the centre for all politics, but unknown to the Japanese, the government had been re-situated in Chungking. Having already taken Peking and Shanghai, the Japanese amassed 300,000 soldiers ready for the Nanking onslaught. Japanese bombs were dropped every night, and for weeks people began to evacuate, beginning with the wealthy and then the middle class. Those who had to stay behind were mainly the very poor and incapacitated.

Ten days later, on 12th December 1937, Nanking fell to the Japanese in one of the most horrendous orgies of murder, rape and plunder ever known in wartime. They killed everyone they saw; no one was spared – even children were used as targets for bayonet practice. According to the Tokyo war trials after the war, at least 20,000 women were raped and killed by Japanese soldiers in the first month of occupation, and soldiers were ordered to kill all prisoners of war.

Records state that an estimated 220,000 Chinese were slaughtered and buried; Japanese soldiers testified that they also disposed of an additional 150,000 bodies.

It was later said that even some of the Japanese officers wept for shame on hearing of the barbarity of their fellow countrymen.

The significance of the massacre is not so much how many people were killed, but the manner in which they were killed. The Japanese soldiers went out of their way to dispose of people in the most brutal fashion: burying people alive, torturing people indiscriminately and raping women in large numbers; something unprecedented in the 20th century.

News of the Nanking rape spread like wildfire and before long refugees were flooding into Shanghai across Suchou Creek and on to the Bund. Thousands upon thousands blocked every street and bridge, clambering to reach the Refugee Zone set up by a catholic priest; it was a seething mass of humanity urged on by fear and the unknown. As the locals poured into Shanghai, the foreigners began to pour out.

With her husband away, Margery was unsure of what to do. The British Consul announced that all British subjects could leave for Hong Kong if they so wished and many of Margery's friends who were leaving urged her to go too. Leonard was up-river and unreachable, so she finally made the decision to leave. There was no time to pack up the apartment, so without a second thought she left the houseboy to crate up everything and send it on to Hong Kong. Thinking back, she realised that she had no idea where he lived or what his proper name was and in the event of anything or everything disappearing, she would not know where to find him. However, as was common in those days with Chinese servants, Ah Lau remained loyal and honest and not a single item was missing when the crates arrived in Hong Kong.

It was at this time that the Japanese sank the American gunboat *Panay* and seriously damaged HMS *Ladybird* – not a very popular move considering their war was, as yet, with China and not with the United States or Great Britain.

* * *

Accommodation had already been arranged for the large group of women and children who travelled on the *Rajputana*, and on arrival in Hong Kong, Margery went to a guest house in Mody Road, Kowloon, owned by Mrs Keller. Hong Kong at the period was booming. The British way of life was secure and prosperous and trade with the rest of the world was inexhaustible – Hong Kong had the busiest harbour in the world, with seagoing vessels, cargo boats, junks and ferries ploughing its waters all day long. Like Shanghai, it was exotic and exciting, with plenty of shops, restaurants and entertainment. Not many of the European civil servants, bankers and merchants had fewer than two or three servants – a cookboy, a wash amah, a houseboy and a baby amah when the children were born, the latter spoiling the children rotten and loving them like a mother.

It was a haven for married women: no housework, no cooking, washing or ironing, and dinner parties were arranged by the number one boy and produced by the cook-boy. The best waiters and barbers, bartenders and man-servants were all Japanese and, as it turned out, the best spies. The *Tai tais* spent their days shopping, not for food, but for the exotic – brocades, silks, jade and rose-quartz figurines, fine porcelain, carved ivory and camphorwood. Life was sweet and there was no reason to believe it would ever change.

As usual Margery could not be idle for long and when she learnt that there was a job vacancy in a shop named the Caravan, she quickly applied. The shop sold Chinese brocades, fine china, Chinese jewellery and pure silk ladies' underwear and was situated in the ground floor arcade of the prestigious Peninsula Hotel. The owner, Eileen Kershaw, (who later became my godmother), re-established the shop after the war in 1947 under her name. Both she and her husband were interned in Stanley Camp, where, sadly, she was to lose her husband. Little did Margery know that she would work there for nearly 30 years and that the shop itself would still be in existence in the 1990s.

* * *

Having returned to Hankow, where air raids were a daily occurrence, Leonard's ship remained there until July, at which time Ministry of Finance guards embarked for a passage to Ichang, which was about 250 miles further up the river. Once embarkation was complete, the officer in charge handed Leonard a list of the troops on board. He had noticed there was a rather large number of female passengers. Enquiring as to how these women should be entered in the logbook (since it was obvious that they should not have been there), the officer, not quite certain how to explain, was relieved when my father suggested he enter them as 'camp followers'.

The Japanese continued to advance along the line of the Yangtze River but with great resistance from the Chinese, who fought hard to restrict rather than defeat them. In January 1938 the Japanese advanced in a southerly direction, making steady progress along the main rail lines, but failed to extend their control laterally. By April they had reached Taierchwang, where they were surrounded by 200,000 Chinese regular and guerrilla troops. They managed to fight their way north out of the encirclement, but it was certainly a great moral booster for the Chinese.

On 29th April 1938 (the birthday of the Emperor of Japan), a huge raid was expected to mark the birthday and this proved to be correct when 19 bombers were shot down over Hankow. The Japanese had recovered their strength and nerve, and again launched more attacks from the north and south and were anxious to extend their territory to the west.

In June 1938 a Chinese expeditionary force moved up the Yellow River with a view to taking the rail junction at Chengchow. It was a strategic point for the Chinese to keep out of the hands of the Japanese as it would seriously affect mobility and supplies for the Chinese forces and leave the way open for an advance on Hankow. The Chinese were in a desperate situation, having to take extreme measures; they broke the banks of the Yellow River, thus diverting it into its original course and flooding vast areas. It was successful and the Japanese offensive was cancelled during July, but it was only a temporary stay, and the Japanese, determined to take Hankow, moved further south so as to be able to move up the line of the Yangtze during July. Chiang was equally determined not to allow the Japanese to take the capital and some of the worst fighting took place in the whole of the Sino-Japanese War. But it was inevitable and Hankow finally fell on 25th October 1938.

Canton also fell to the Japanese in the autumn and within a year they controlled most of the ports that accounted for 90 per cent of the revenue. In spite of this, the service continued to function and the Japanese authorities regularly dispersed quotas for the expenses of the CMC Inspectorate while keeping the bulk for themselves.

A week after safely arriving in Ichang with Finance Ministry guards, Leonard was relieved of his command and boarded one of Jardine's river steamers to return to Hankow. But the Japanese had blocked the Yangtze River, so he was unable to continue by boat. By this time the railway between Wuchang (the town on the opposite side of the river) and Canton had been cut in several places by Japanese air raids, so after waiting a week for a train which on arrival was completely booked anyway, he again had to wait another day for the next train. This did not seem to make any difference time-wise as his train eventually caught up with the first one which had had a day's start in Shakwan (then capital of Kwangtung). Bombed bridges had been repaired with masses of bamboo so it was not very consoling to think that his train had to follow the first one across, which may have already strained the bridge to breaking point. In Shakwan another coach was added to the rear of the train, which was then shunted into a tunnel where they were to spend the day. Under cover of darkness the train then proceeded to Lokchuan on the North River, where passengers were transferred to river craft. First- and second-class passengers were accommodated in a small motor riverboat which towed third-class passengers in four local wooden junks.

By this time my father had met a missionary doctor from the Methodist Hospital in Shakwan who spoke fluent Cantonese, which was to prove most useful. During the day the steamers holed up in river ports as protection against the Japanese bombers, moving on at night, and eventually reaching Canton on a Sunday morning. Leonard immediately booked into the Victoria Hotel in Shameen (the International Settlement), where he was able to have a long-awaited hot bath and a much-needed beer.

He was already in the bath when the room boy shouted out, 'Have got beer, master' … to which my father replied, 'Please bring it in here', which rather surprised the chap. It was the first and only time he drank in a bath!

Later that day he telephoned Margery, who had been anxiously awaiting his arrival in Hong Kong. He then reported to the Canton Commissioner, Lester Little, an American (later to become the last Western Inspector General of the Chinese Customs), who suggested that he wait until the next day and go on to Hong Kong by river steamer, which would have been less hazardous than the train. Leonard did not warm to that idea very much since he had not seen his wife for 13 months and he was only 92 miles away.

HONG KONG

Due to the Sino-Japanese War in China, 13 Customs vessels had been moved to Hong Kong and laid up in the harbour. The Japanese had imposed a naval blockade on the whole of the coast and trade could only be continued by foreign-flag vessels. By 1939 the Japanese had taken the ports of Swatow, Amoy, Foochow and Wenchow as well as Hainan Island (a tropical island off the southernmost tip of China). Hainan was of great geographical importance to the Chinese Customs. All ocean-going junks from Saigon, Singapore and Bangkok had to report to Hoihow on the island before sailing to any mainland port in China. It was an area which attracted large-scale contraband, which was landed in Fort Bayard, a dormant French enclave leased from the Ching Empire in 1898, and then shipped across to Hainan. The Customs continued to operate to the best of their ability but many of the ships had been seized by the Japanese, who made increasing demands regarding the disposal of revenue collection. Certain members of the Chinese Government wanted the Customs to abandon the occupied ports and move the staff more inland to new stations but the Commissioner was loath to do this, pointing out that it would give the Japanese complete economic control over the whole area they occupied. Under the terms of the Treaty between Britain and China covering the Leased Territories held by Britain on a 99-year lease, China retained the right for commissioned ships to navigate the waters around Hong Kong and the Leased Territories.

The Chinese Customs had a number of stations on the

north coast of Mirs Bay and Deep Bay, but communications between the two had become difficult, owing to the soldiers not being paid and consequently ganging up with smugglers as armed escorts. As a result, Leonard was sent out to Mirs Bay as Acting First Officer in charge of CPS (Customs Preventive Ship) *Kuanchuan* – a 60-ft steel single-screw launch, and far too small to carry anything larger than a sampan.

On 29th July 1939, Leonard received a message that a patrol had made a seizure of wood oil (a hugely profitable export) and he was requested to proceed to the beach to embark the patrol. Having ordered the boat away to the beach, Leonard sat in a deck chair and closed his eyes while waiting for their return. Suddenly he was rudely jolted out of his chair by the sound of bullets hitting the armour-plated wheelhouse behind him. They were being fired on from the shore. It was too dangerous for crew members to go forward and weigh anchor but fortunately the engine was still manned, so Leonard ordered 'full astern' … dragging the anchor and boat out of firing range.

The next problem was to recover his crew from the shore. The water was too shallow to go between the boat and beach but he had to make an immediate decision as his men were hanging on the gunwale of the seaward side of the boat. The only answer was to steam alongside and pull them out of the water. By that time all metal flaps were down over the wheelhouse windows, turning it into a virtual conning tower, with only the rifle ports open. Using constant rifle fire, Leonard had hoped to keep the smugglers' escort pinned down so that the patrol could retire. The exchange of fire continued for well over an hour, during which time the second officer, who was standing next to Leonard, was killed instantly by a bullet entering one of the rifle ports.

Four hours later my father and his crew were able to procure another sampan and rescue the patrol. One crewman was dead and two were wounded; only one man was wounded in the patrol, a bullet glanced off his jaw, taking a slice out of his neck and exposing the jugular vein.

The following morning, having landed the dead and wounded and cleaned up the boat, father discovered that they had been hit no less than 187 times. He was later decorated for his actions by the Commissioner and was one of only two officers ever to receive this Chinese Maritime Customs award.

After this incident which proved that the *Kuanchuan* and other boats like her were too small for that type of work, Leonard was given CPS *Kwanlin* – a 30-ft composite twin-screw vessel with a ram bow, built at the end of the previous century. He was to command her until July 1940, at which time it became obvious that the Japanese were advancing to the border of Hong Kong and China, and the stations were closed down.

On 16th November 1939 while playing bridge with friends, Margery began her labour pains. At 6 p.m. she was bundled into a rickshaw and at the speed of lightning (the rickshaw coolie was not about to become a midwife) and rather shaken, she arrived at Kowloon Hospital, Argyle Street, where I was born at 8 p.m. on the dot. My father saw me at a week old when he returned from a patrol, and I was christened at St Andrew's Church, Nathan Road, a month later.

I was just eight months old when the Hong Kong Government ordered all non-essential foreign women and children to leave Hong Kong on 7th July 1940, and that meant mother and me. Many managed to dodge the evacuation by joining the VADs (Volunteer Aid Detachment – nurses), part of the Hong Kong Volunteer Defence Force, or the Auxiliary Nursing Service. The VADs nursed in military hospitals, the ANSs in civilian hospitals, and all did an excellent job when the invasion started 17 months later. Many lived to regret their decision when they found themselves interned by the Japanese in Stanley Civilian Internment Camp.

It was a difficult and very emotional time for all concerned, especially for the wives leaving their menfolk, not knowing when or if they would ever see them again. Each person was allowed one small suitcase with bare essentials. Ironically, it was the *Empress of Japan* that was to carry us to the Philippines. She had been reconditioned as a troopship and every public room and spare space had been turned into dormitories crammed with camp beds. Mothers with several children were allotted cabins with other families, whereas mothers with a single baby were given a camp bed in one of the public rooms. There was no provision for babies so my mother had to cradle me in her arms while sleeping. Meals were served in the dining saloon in several sittings, which meant that mother would feed me first and then hand me over to someone whilst she had her meal.

The voyage only took 36 hours but because it was the typhoon season, it was very rough at sea and most people were seasick. On arrival in the Philippines we were met by friendly American marines who loaded us up on to army trucks and drove us to Fort Mackinley some miles outside Manila. The accommodation was basic but clean, with brand new camp beds, bedding and mosquito nets. After several days, many of the evacuees were moved to other accommodation to make way for two more shiploads of women and children, but my mother and I stayed (possibly to make it easier for mothers with babies). Some of those who were moved found themselves in undesirable places. One group was placed in an hotel which had been a brothel in the historic walled city of Interamuros. Apart from bedbugs, rats and cockroaches at night, they were also disturbed by potential 'customers'. Fortunately the Red Cross was able to arrange for alternative accommodation but it was a difficult time for all concerned.

There was nothing to do during this waiting period, which posed dreadful problems for mothers with very young children, particularly as it was the rainy season. They could not play outside and trying to dry nappies and clothes was a nightmare.

Some evacuees began to receive letters from loved ones in Hong Kong but there was no mention of any forthcoming trouble and many began to wonder why they were in the Philippines at all. Eventually, because of the long wait and uncomfortable conditions in the Philippines, many women (some with children) very unwisely decided to return to Hong Kong and were consequently interned in the camps. This was to cause a great deal of friction with other internees, who felt that they were an unnecessary burden on the very limited food supplies.

Six weeks from the date of arrival we were once more on a ship, bound for Australia.

In late October 1940, Leonard was ordered to report to the Area Commander and was told that he had been appointed Senior Instructor in the Maritime School of the Customs College,which had been evacuated from Shanghai to Hong Kong University. He was none too happy about this as he felt he was not qualified enough to do the work but there was no one else who could do it, so he found himself frantically studying to keep ahead of the cadets. This was to be his last job before he entered the internment camp at Stanley.

By 1941 the Customs fleet was further reduced by six ships requisitioned by the Royal Navy but, due to difficulties in re-armament, the vessels were never actually commissioned into the Royal Navy. CPS *Chunhsing* became an accommodation ship in Hong Kong and ended her days scuttled across the entrance to Victoria Harbour. The Japanese eventually had to cut her into three parts before they could clear the entrance. Other ships were scuttled on 19th December 1941 but were salvaged by the Japanese and used in various capacities. None of the ships was recovered at the end of the war.

Although an attack on Hong Kong had been expected for a long time, it came as a shock to hear on Manila Radio at 7.30 a.m. on 8th December 1941 that Pearl Harbour had been attacked by the Japanese and that a state of war existed. The previous day, Sunday, had been like any other in the Far East. It was a day for pleasure and relaxation – curry 'tiffins', swimming parties, golf, cricket, sailing, dinners and dancing – a normal day for Europeans in the tropics.

However, that morning during the church service, General Maltby, General Officer Commanding in Hong Kong was called outside. The observation posts of the 2/14 Punjabis reported the massing of Japanese troops north of Fanling in the New Territories. General Maltby called an emergency conference of all unit commanders and ordered that by 5 p.m. that day, all soldiers, sailors and Hong Kong Volunteer Defence Corps personnel must be at battle stations.

Using the Star Ferry to cross the harbour for work that Monday morning, Leonard met up with one of the Chinese Customs outdoor staff he had known since his days in Hankow. He was halfway across the harbour and in the middle of relaying the morning news when at precisely 8 a.m. the air raid siren sounded. Some passengers remarked that it was just the usual drill, but soon changed their minds when the first bombs dropped on Kai Tak aerodrome, knocking out the only five planes the local air force possessed: three obsolete torpedo bombers and two old amphibians. It was all over in five minutes and the Japanese, flushed with such quick success, dropped leaflets all over the Colony, but the recipients were not impressed. It was the beginning of 17 days of success and failure, elation and despair, and useless loss of lives.

On the afternoon of 11th December, the Japanese had advanced about 15 miles towards the outskirts of Kowloon. Bumping into the Chief Tide Surveyor and his wife, my father was told that everyone should proceed to the Island of Hong Kong.

'Oh, Captain Williams,' said the surveyor's wife, 'will you do us a favour? Will you do something about Bolly? We don't want him to fall into the hands of the Japanese.'

Not knowing who or what Bolly was, Leonard was introduced to a parrot in a cage. After some hesitation he covered the parrot with his hat and did the only humane thing possible.

'Is Bolly all right?'

Leonard assured her that all was well – he too did not want to think of Bolly falling into Japanese hands.

Shortly after that Leonard did his duty as a rickshaw coolie! One of the numerous wives, who by then should have been in Australia, was allegedly too sick to walk to the Star Ferry – a distance of less than half a mile. Most of the rickshaw coolies had fled, so there was no shortage of free rickshaws. As he headed towards the ferry with the passenger in tow, he had a near miss when someone took a shot at him with a rifle. It was a local about to change sides!

The following weeks were spent going around hospitals and dugouts with food and supplies. It was to have been the job of the beautifully uniformed ARP staff but, under the pressure, they had simply disappeared. Once when Leonard asked a gang to help load coal onto a lorry, they too disappeared, stating that they were not coolies. He finally found a good gang of locals who remained with him until the day before surrender on Christmas Day 1941 when they were almost killed by a mortar shell.

Finally in October 1940, after having left Hong Kong in July, mother and I arrived in Sydney after a very delayed stopover in the Philippines, where we had to wait for a Dutch (neutral) ship to take us on to Australia. On arrival we were put in an hotel for the night before catching a train to Adelaide, where my paternal grandparents were now living.

In early December Margery's brother Tom, who was a lieutenant commander in the Royal Navy, arrived in Sydney Harbour and phoned to give her news of Hong Kong and the likelihood that it was about to fall to the Japanese. For security reasons he was unable to tell her when he would next be in Sydney, so he would send a postcard suggesting she had lunch with friends on a certain date, and this would be the clue. After meeting her brother in Sydney and then returning to Adelaide, Margery realised that she would get a great deal more news of the war in the Far East and Pacific if she were permanently in Sydney, and so, with her in-laws' approval, we moved there.

One of the biggest problems for my mother was that she had no income and in order to survive she would need to get a job. One day, while I was crawling around the sand on Bondi Beach, she got talking to a woman and mentioned that she was looking for work. The woman said she would see what she could do as her husband was head of the Standard-Vacuum Oil Co. and she would find out if there were any vacancies. A few days later my mother was interviewed in the morning and by the afternoon was already at work, where she was to stay, and spend many happy hours, until my father was released from the Japanese prison camp after the war.

In spite of this, life was not easy for my mother. I was

one and a half years old and unable to be left alone at home.

Mrs Ball, who had left Shanghai with two daughters and two Chinese amahs, was taking in children to board while mothers had to work. It was not an ideal situation but the only answer in the circumstances, and for the next couple of years mother and I were only to see each other from Saturday lunchtime to Sunday evening. It must have been a very difficult and emotional time for her, especially since she received little or no news of my father in Hong Kong, and it was not much fun for me as I was dragged, kicking and screaming, back to Mrs Ball's every Sunday night. The first year my mother did hear from father twice when he was allowed to send a postcard containing 25 words, but these were censored anyway by the Japanese. He was unable to give any real news but at least she knew he was still alive. Thereafter she heard nothing even though she herself tried many ways of getting mail to him.

Margery found the Australian people very kind and sympathetic to her situation and her colleagues at work were more than helpful. After the war, her boss, Mr Cottie, was reluctant to let her go and suggested she take a holiday and then return. It was a nice gesture but Leonard had to return to work and so we left Australia for a brief stay in the UK.

HONG KONG FALLS

By 1941 the Japanese had more or less done what they had set out to do in China and their attention was now turned to the British and Dutch in South East Asia and the Americans in the Pacific.

At the beginning of January 1942, all foreigners who were not already POWs were rounded up and accommodated in various hotels and brothels for about three weeks before being transported to Stanley Peninsula on the south side of Hong Kong Island, where an internment camp had been established at St Stephen's College.

St Stephen's College, a well-known seat of learning for 30 years, had already been made into a makeshift hospital to house the many men badly wounded during the fighting – men with gaping stomach and chest wounds, faces blown away, limbs blown off and every imaginable wound possible: there were no malingerers in that hospital. The devoted nursing staff, a British nursing sister from the British Military Hospital, six British VADs, four Chinese nurses and several medical orderlies, did all they could to alleviate the horrendous pain without blood transfusions, very little morphine and hardly any first aid equipment.

Prior to the Japanese landing, a well-known and respected Hong Kong doctor, George Black, was put in command of this hospital at St Stephen's College. He had seen a great deal of action in the First World War and had ribbons to prove it. On Christmas Day 1941 patients awoke as usual at 5.34 a.m. and Colonel Dr George Black issued every patient with a tot (he had provided a crate of liquor himself). By 6 a.m. six Winnipeg Grenadiers entered the hospital to inform the doctor that the Japanese were heading their way and to evacuate the patients quickly.

Because of the severity of the wounds, Dr Black said evacuation was impossible and pointing to the fluttering Red Cross flag on the roof said, 'That is our protection, we'll be all right.' He then told the Canadians to leave quickly, but not before issuing them all with a double whisky each. Little did Black know that many of the 200 Japanese advancing towards St Stephen's were drunk and out of control and were not about to respect the Red Cross flag.

'This is a hospital,' said Black as he placed his arm across the door, barring their way. The two lead soldiers grinned, took aim and shot him through the head. Not satisfied with that, they then bayoneted Dr Black a dozen or more times. This was followed by bandages being ripped off the patients, who were then also bayoneted. The nurses could do nothing but stand by helplessly – one nurse even threw herself across a patient and was bayoneted with the man in bed. In half an hour 56 wounded men were mercilessly slaughtered, while a few managed to hide under their beds until it was all over.

The soldiers then turned their attention to the nurses in their blood-spattered uniforms; they were roughly rounded up and taken away. Their fate is unmentionable.

A similar act of extreme barbarity was to be repeated at the Jockey Club in Happy Valley, again because of drunken, undisciplined soldiers under the command of junior officers, although on this occasion the nurses were raped but not murdered.

STANLEY CAMP

The mixed camp of men, women and children was made up of about 3,500 people of different nationalities: Americans, Canadians, Dutch, Belgian and some Norwegians, with the majority being British.

Because of its geographical situation, the choice of Stanley Peninsula on the south side of Hong Kong Island, was the perfect place for an internment camp. On three sides was water: Tytam Bay, Stanley Bay and Tweed Bay, all of which had been popular for beach parties and swimming. There was one road which led to the city of Victoria and, to the south west, a road which led to the Stanley Garrison, soon to billet the Japanese garrison. To the north east the road cut through the camp to a dead end at Stanley Prison. From there a narrow path led down left to the isolated Tweed Bay Hospital behind which was a small building known as the Leprosarium. This housed the medical staff but later was used as a sanatorium for TB cases. The path continued past the hospital and ended at the Indian Quarters, which housed married couples and singles all crowded together. It was completely cut off from the remainder of the Island.

The prison area had been formerly occupied by prison staff. There were warders' married and single quarters, Indian warders' quarters, a hospital, a cemetery and a prison officers' clubhouse. St Stephen's College, with boarding facilities and bungalows for the staff and families, was also included in the area, and up the hill, strategically placed, were the houses and gardens of the Commissioner and Deputy Commissioner of Prisons, where the Japanese Commandant and his staff installed themselves. To the south west where the road branched off to the garrison was a large playing field where, during the early months, POWs were allowed to exercise until a few escaped. The field was later used for growing vegetables.

The four main blocks for housing were the pre-war Married Quarters, Indian Quarters, Dutch Quarters and American Quarters. To the north of these was St Stephen's College. Above the classrooms were dormitories and cubicles. The main building, which was in an H shape, had a large concert hall in the centre and, for single or unattached men, accommodation was far better than for those in the main blocks. Many of these men were professionals or academics, ships' officers and engineers with ages ranging from 20 to 70. As a group they could always be relied upon to pull their weight and shared enthusiastically in responsibilities and duties in the camp. They achieved a degree of independence and self-sufficiency and maintained a certain cheerfulness. Most seemed more able to accept their situation – perhaps because, unlike many others, they knew that their families were safe elsewhere. It was very much the case with my father.

Once inside the camp, Leonard discovered that the

upstairs cubicles contained two or three hospital beds and one or two pieces of furniture, which was a great bonus. He had no need for them as he had brought in a canvas camp bed so he distributed them to the women in the Married Quarters.

To the south and just beyond the sports field was the cemetery – a place that was to become all too familiar to Leonard. Surrounded by casuarina trees, it had quietly existed for over a century until the burial of the massacred doctors and nurses, together with some of the dead soldiers who had died in the Stanley area during the Defence of Hong Kong in 1941, had disturbed it once more. It was a place where internees would quietly sit and contemplate their fate, where lovers would meet or where solace was sought. A place in which few Japanese would venture. And it still exists today, quietly undisturbed, with its grim reminder and secrets of Hong Kong's cruel occupation.

By the middle of February 1942, the bulk of internees were in the camp and nearly all the accommodation was grossly overcrowded. Changes were made so that families could now be housed together. Priority was given to hospital, administrative and kitchen staff who could not be fitted into the hospital buildings.

A camp office was set up in the Married Quarters where Mr Franklin Gimson (Representative of Internees) was based. Mr Gimson was a newly arrived (December 1941) civil servant who had been posted to Hong Kong on the eve of the Japanese invasion.

The son of a Leicestershire clergyman, he was married to a clergyman's daughter and had spent his previous 27 years' colonial service in Ceylon. Fortunately, his wife and two daughters were unable to join him from England because of the war there, and Gimson had barely time to introduce himself to Hong Kong's Governor, Sir Mark Young, when Hong Kong surrendered on Christmas Day to the Japanese.

In due course Franklin Gimson, the only senior government official remaining (Sir Mark Young was taken to China), was also interned in Stanley, where he was subjected to insults and hostility from many of his own countrymen. Because Gimson had newly arrived in the Colony, he had taken no part in the decisions of the Government and yet they blamed the defeat on the Government's inability to defend the Colony and vented their bitterness and venom on him. Many British thought they should be repatriated to Britain at once and again blamed Gimson when he rightly pointed out that it was impossible.

He was a man of immense integrity with a sense of purpose that never wavered throughout the 44 months of sickness, humiliation, misery and hunger – a man who stood up against Japanese authority when necessary and often had his requests granted; it was through this that he began to establish himself as the leader and spokesman for all internees.

Without the courage, resolve and outward optimism of this little-known civil servant who never shared in Hong Kong's spectacular profits, Hong Kong would have immediately reverted to China in 1945.

Unknown to Britain, President Roosevelt had promised Chiang Kai-shek that since Hong Kong was in China's area of influence, arrangements for the Japanese surrender and administration would be made by him as there was no certainty that Hong Kong would continue to be British. Roosevelt wanted Hong Kong to be a free port, which would have been very advantageous to American trade. Obviously no one had told him that Hong Kong had been leased to the British for 99 years!

After the war Gimson was knighted for his services to Hong Kong and within months of repatriation, returned to Singapore as Governor.

* * *

During the first weeks in Stanley, everyone familiarised themselves with the layout of the camp and cleaned up much of the damage that had occurred during the siege of Hong Kong. Many buildings had been hit by bombs and shelling by the Japanese, although the flats themselves were still intact.

Leonard, together with other 'single' men, was detailed to clean up the camp and repair roads etc. The essential services were first priority, one of them being the sanitary disposal team, of which father was also a part. With water rationing, it was a difficult task to keep the toilets emptied and clean, particularly as time went on when more and more internees suffered from bad dysentery and intestinal problems.

Prior to the war there had been an anti-malarial campaign in Hong Kong, which was just beginning to have some effect when the Japanese took over. Their neglect not only ruined years of work, but also had a serious effect on prisoners. Mosquitoes began to breed in the badly damaged and unserviceable reservoirs, in undrained pools and in heaps of garbage on the streets. Stanley Peninsula, where the internees were located, should have been relatively free of mosquitoes, but barbed wire is no deterrent to these insects and they swarmed all over the Colony, causing great problems for the prisoners. There was little or no quinine to be had.

One of the ongoing problems was bed bugs. They would hide themselves in and behind everything. Leonard with his canvas bed was continually removing the cross bars which slotted through the canvas to hold it in place. Inside these cavities, clusters of moving black bodies were to be found, each one fat with blood. The only way to get rid of them was to squash them as quickly as possible – when squashed, they exuded a sickly smell of bitter almonds.

His next job was the unpleasant task of digging graves. Obviously there were no coffins available for funerals, so an old wardrobe with a false bottom was requisitioned for the purpose. It was used for every funeral except two, and because of this wardrobe, the graves had to be 7 ft 6 in long, 4 ft 7 in, wide and 4 ft 6 in deep – not an enviable job at any time let alone when the earth was baked hard like concrete and almost impenetrable.

'After digging, sometimes for a whole day, we would knock off once ground level was in line with my left nipple. That made it exactly four feet six inches deep,' he said. Graves were usually dug well in advance so there was always one ready, often used by lovers, knowing full well no Japanese would venture into the graveyard at night. However, several people who did not have to do the back-breaking work thought it too depressing to see open graves while attending a funeral, and complained. Consequently pre-dug graves were suspended – this was to eventually backfire.

One day, just after starting a new grave for a recent demise, the grave diggers were on their way to their mid-day meal when they were informed of a burial at 3 p.m. – someone had passed away suddenly, which was not uncommon.

'Sorry,' said Leonard, 'he'll have to wait, there is no grave ready.' As a result pre-dug graves were the policy once more.

Often during the summer months when the humidity was extreme, so too the temperatures, the internees would move their beds outside and sleep in the open. One morning an internee who had done just that said that he had been woken in the night by the hot breath of a panting animal in his face; he said it was a tiger. Since tigers were not natural animals in Hong Kong, most people just thought he was either going off his head or had imagined the whole incident. A few days later another internee said he had spotted a tiger and again there was disbelief. Most thought it may have been a rather large dog until pug marks were seen on yet another occasion. The Japanese authorities were informed and they immediately sent for some Indian soldier prisoners from a Kowloon camp, who finally managed to track the large cat to the Stanley Fort area, where it was killed. It was indeed a tiger. The carcase was then taken into Victoria, where the dairy farm butcher brought from Stanley Camp, was asked to skin it. On making enquiries as to where the tiger had come from, it was thought that someone had released it from a circus in Causeway Bay.

Food

When prisoners were first interned, two small meals a day were provided which consisted of a small quantity of rice and scraps of vegetables and sometimes unmarketable fish. After a month of such rations the Japanese authorities had the audacity to present the internees with a bill for $86,000 for their accommodation and food, which also included their own sojourn in the hotels and brothels prior to entering the camp! After a special meeting with the various British camp officials, it was decided that the account would be paid by cheque (to keep the Japanese happy) against a guarantee to be met by a future British Government. However, the cheque was returned by the Japanese as British funds were frozen.

Six months into camp life, Leonard was detailed as cook in the kitchen of his block – another unenviable job for anyone who was conscious of the appalling hunger that everyone felt, and the bickering that accompanied it.

The Japanese did not supply kitchen equipment, so a 20-gallon boiler and three pans were all he had to cook for about 85 people on a wood fire, supplemented with dry grass. Meal times varied according to whether there was enough firewood available but they did try to keep to around 12 noon and 5 p.m. The food, too, varied considerably, as did the quality of rice, which was often full of dirt and gravel. Rations consisted of 1½ ounces of meat *a week* with 8 ounces of rice per day. It was difficult to equalise the rations in this way, so more than often it was made into a stew, and the monotony of this, with cold rice, did not excite much interest!

Rice initially fills the stomach but soon turns to water, and hunger sets in once more.

For the first couple of months flour was provided and bread was baked by many of the blocks in makeshift ovens. When flour was no longer available 'rice bread' was baked and one small, but apparently delicious, slice was distributed daily.

Lack of salt caused many to have muscular cramps, so after complaining to the authorities they were allowed to collect sea water for cooking. This helped alleviate the cramps as well as improving the taste of the rice and whatever else there was.

Sometimes fish was provided (but it was often far from fresh), and then fried in whatever oil was left, which was usually very, very rancid.

The distribution of the food was a difficult task and always a worry to my father, who would almost rather go without than be accused of having more than his due.

Every now and then an eel was brought in to be cooked and he would wonder how he was going to divide it fairly between 85 people. The answer was to boil it so that it disintegrated and then distribute a portion of the fleshy soup to everyone – at least they would have the goodness that way. Often fish was dipped in a type of rice batter to conceal the small amount. A ration from the tail end appeared large at about 1½ inches long, whereas a piece from behind the gills would be small at about half an inch thick. One particularly selfish internee, and there were plenty of them, was always whingeing and asking for larger portions. He wanted the tail piece; when he discovered that it was mostly bone he soon stopped his complaining and learnt to be thankful for what he had.

Sweet potatoes were a delicacy providing the much needed source of energy, sugar. These were grown in patches around the camp. However, most of the time potatoes were well and truly rotten – not even fit for pigs – so what there was had to be carefully peeled; the slightest piece of rotten potato permeated the whole stew.

Leonard was just about running out of his very limited cooking ideas when he was asked to teach navigation to a small class of seafarers who had been captured by the Japanese – a job to which he felt far better suited. Shortage of paper was the biggest problem although the Japanese supplied sheets of very coarse brown paper complete with large wooden splinters. His lectures were first written on this paper and then, after removing the offending splinters, he used the paper for what it was originally intended – the toilet!

Still, food was always on people's minds and a constant source of worry. It didn't matter what the topic of conversation was, it would always turn to food. It was impossible to describe the physical hunger endured in the early days of camp and throughout. The impact of continuous hunger on people is profound. George Orwell, who saw starving tramps between the wars, said, 'Hunger reduces one to an utterly spineless, brainless condition . . . as though all one's blood had been pumped out and lukewarm water substituted.'*

It was not only the POWs who ate everything and anything they could get hold of, but also internees developed the same capacity – they were the survivors. They consumed snakes, grasshoppers, maggots, weeds, dogs, cats, grass – anything that either moved or grew. There were as many problems from the internees regarding food as there were from the Japanese, who never hesitated to withhold

---

*George Orwell: *Down and Out in Paris and London*

distribution of parcels as a punishment for the smallest breach of law such as failing to bow to a sentry.

It cannot be stressed enough how difficult it was to get individual parcels to POWs in the Far East. There was the uncertainty of ships ever arriving at their destination as well as Japanese reluctance at the highest levels. Prior to April 1945, 225,000 private parcels for POWs and internees were dispatched and received in the Far East. Although this may sound a great deal, it actually meant one parcel per person, if fairly distributed, since there were as many POWs.

After the war, evidence emerged at the war trials that many thousands of private and Red Cross parcels were stockpiled by the Japanese, against some future need, until August 1945, as well as many being pillaged by them. Very few individual parcels ever got through – mother sent five, out of which my father received one in the early days of internment.

The biggest problem for the Red Cross authorities with the Japanese military was the fact that the Japanese refused point blank to abide by the Geneva Convention. Colonel Count Tokunaga, the Camp Commander, when reminded of the Convention would fly into a rage – they were not subject to the Convention!

The Japanesc had no excuse for starving the prisoners. The British Government had remitted, through the Red Cross, £10,000 every month for the relief of civilians, internees and war prisoners. Adequate food stores had been established all over Hong Kong Island for such an emergency, but instead of giving it to the prisoners and others in town, the food was shipped to Japan.

There were two godowns in the camp with enough food in them to last everyone for six months, but it was never distributed. The thought of all that food inside the godowns was too much for some, who organised systematic night raids. At first, mainly tinned goods were taken – corned beef, soups and butter – all for their own use, but once someone managed to sell a tin they realised there was a fortune to be made exploiting other internees. At one stage 240-lb bags of rice were pinched which they hid under their beds. It was not difficult to see who the culprits were as their sudden affluence was obvious to all.

Internees kept themselves going by looking forward to Red Cross supplies, but only three consignments ever reached the camp: one from Britain in June 1942 (this was held by the Japanese for three months before distribution), two comfort parcels, followed by a six-month bulk supply of tinned meat, tea, cocoa, sugar and dried fruit which was distributed each month till it ran out.

The Americans were repatriated in June 1942 and the Canadians in September 1943. At this time the Canadian Red Cross sent three parcels for each person in the camp but no bulk supplies. By the time the last consignment reached the camp in February 1945, most of the internees were starving.

Rumours of more supplies from the American Red Cross grossly exaggerated the size and weight of the parcels and raised people's hopes for a bumper parcel. They were bitterly disappointed when they eventually received a small parcel each (these were left over from the 1942 British Red Cross consignment), containing chocolate and cheese covered in green mould, and rusted, bloated tins of meat and fruit. The American Red Cross parcels that were to have been delivered to Stanley Camp were shipped to Japan instead. A number of internees who had been employees of Jardines, Shell, BAT and Butterfield and Swire received regular parcels from outside the camp, which caused a great deal of friction from those who got nothing. Many thought the parcels should be shared between the other 3,000 internees even though it was less than 10 per cent who received them.

It seems that the Japanese were determined to starve the

prisoners (possibly to death), and starve they certainly did. As a result of a prolonged deficiency in the diet of thiamine and vitamin B, many contracted severe beriberi, not only in Stanley Camp but also in Sham Shui Po, Ma Tau Chung and Argyle Street camps.

Sickness

There were two forms of beriberi in Stanley – dry and wet. Wet beriberi was less painful but more hazardous to life because of the swelling caused by the retention of large amounts of fluid in the body (oedema). It usually began in the feet and progressed up the body; if it reached the heart, death was likely to occur.

In the dry form there was no swelling but extreme pain, usually confined to the feet, legs and hands, and the patient was apathetic and dull.

Another chronically painful and rather strange complaint that many internees suffered from was 'burning feet syndrome'. It usually became more painful at night and was exacerbated by heat – those affected could do little to alleviate the discomfort except place the feet in cold water. Again it was obviously caused by deficiency in the meagre diet on which they were all forced to exist.

The third most common disease was pellagra. This affects the skin, gut and brain – the disease of the three Ds, i.e. dermatitis, diarrhoea and dementia. However, it can exist without these three symptoms, making diagnosis very difficult. Failing vision, painful feet and frequent emptying of the bladder could also be symptoms, but the most serious feature of pellagra is mental disturbance and dementia. The most severe cases all died in camp.

Amazingly, with all the health problems that existed, there were no suicides in Stanley Camp. However, it was not uncommon for men and women to just give up and die, not because they were sick but because they had had enough. They just lost the will to live.

In total, fewer than 130 prisoners died. In August 1943, Sir Vandeleur Grayburn who was Head of the Hong Kong and Shanghai Banking Corporation in Hong Kong, was arrested, imprisoned and tortured. The Japs accused him of being the leader of an espionage ring responsible for smuggling British Army Aid Group Intelligence messages and money into the camp. He died in Stanley Prison Hospital on 22nd August.

Seven were executed on the beach at Stanley in October 1943 including the former Defence Secretary, J. A. Fraser, and D. W. Waterton who were accused of being involved in operating a secret radio set in camp, and fourteen were killed by allied planes in January 1945 in a most unfortunate incident at St Stephen's College. Along the main road leading towards Stanley Fort was a Japanese mobile anti-aircraft gun which allied planes were targeting. Sadly the bombs went way off course and landed right next to some bungalows.

Up until early August 1945, my father had kept amazingly well for all his 6 stone (84 lb) body weight, then he began to experience severe pains under his right rib cage. He was climbing onto the work truck one day when he had a sudden acute attack of pain and fell to the ground. Seeing a Japanese guard approaching, he closed his eyes expecting a kick or a rifle butt. He waited for the moment . . . it never came. To his amazement the guard pulled him to his feet and threw him onto the truck. Perhaps he had seen the genuine pain . . . perhaps he was one of the kinder ones (there were a few). Who knows? Leonard was eventually sent to the camp hospital, where the doctor diagnosed gall stones. He was hospitalised and the surgeon indicated that if it did not improve he would have to operate. Not something anyone would want to undertake. To ensure that everything was

Parents wedding at the Holy Trinity Cathedral Shanghai 10th October 1936.

My father as 2nd Officer on CLT *Haihsing*, 1936.

海關關員檢查憑照

爲發給憑照事，茲按照海關緝私條例第一第二兩條之規定，派本關關員魏禮仕執行緝私職務，該員得於關係場所、船舶、航空機、車輛等查緝私貨，並得搜索認爲有違犯緝私條例情事者之身體，准以合法行爲，切實執行緝私條例，及海關定章。此照

右給魏禮仕收執

中華民國叁拾陸年弍月　日

九龍關稅務司

附註：關員於執行職務期間必須隨身攜帶此項憑照

My father's Chinese Maritime Customs Certificate of authority in Chinese.

The amah holding me at 1 month old.

1939 Father receiving the Customs silver medal for bravery (only 2 men ever received this).

Father with crew of CPS *Kuanchuan* being commended by the Superintendent.

My mother and I on arrival in Australia after being evacuated.

My mother (right) selling Red Cross flags in Sydney 1942.

Up the Yangtse River.

An improvised kitchen in Stanley Civilian Prison Camp where my father worked for a while.

Internees grinding rice.

My father with natives of Hainan Island.

Post war - Japanese naval prisoners being used as labourers.

Hong Kong harbour in 1945

The Peninsula Hotel where we resided from 1947-1951.

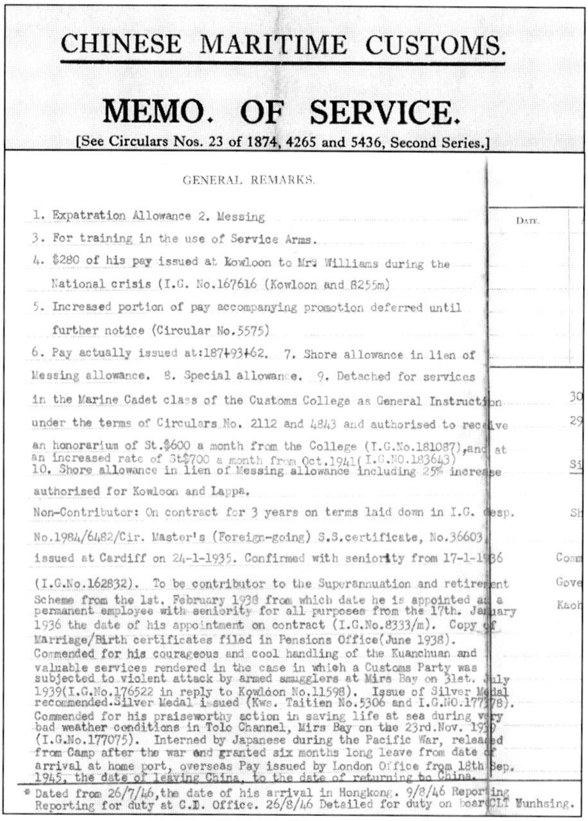

CHINESE MARITIME CUSTOMS.

MEMO. OF SERVICE.

[See Circulars Nos. 23 of 1874, 4265 and 5436, Second Series.]

GENERAL REMARKS.

1. Expatration Allowance 2. Messing
3. For training in the use of Service Arms.
4. $280 of his pay issued at Kowloon to Mrs Williams during the National crisis (I.G. No.167616 (Kowloon and 8255m)
5. Increased portion of pay accompanying promotion deferred until further notice (Circular No.5575)
6. Pay actually issued at:187+93+62. 7. Shore allowance in lien of Messing allowance. 8. Special allowance. 9. Detached for services in the Marine Cadet class of the Customs College as General Instruction under the terms of Circulars No. 2112 and 4843 and authorised to receive an honorarium of St.$600 a month from the College (I.G.No.181087),and at an increased rate of St$700 a month from Oct.1941(I.G.NO.183643)
10. Shore allowance in lien of Messing allowance including 25% increase authorised for Kowloon and Lappa.

Non-Contributor: On contract for 3 years on terms laid down in I.G. desp. No.1984/6482/Cir. Master's (Foreign-going) S.S.certificate, No.36603, issued at Cardiff on 24-1-1935. Confirmed with seniority from 17-1-1936 (I.G.No.162832). To be contributor to the Superannuation and retirement Scheme from the 1st. February 1938 from which date he is appointed as a permanent employee with seniority for all purposes from the 17th. January 1936 the date of his appointment on contract (I.G.No.8333/m). Copy of Marriage/Birth certificates filed in Pensions Office(June 1938). Commended for his courageous and cool handling of the Kuanchuan and valuable services rendered in the case in which a Customs Party was subjected to violent attack by armed smugglers at Mirs Bay on 31st. July 1939(I.G.No.176522 in reply to Kowloon No.11598). Issue of Silver Medal recommended.Silver Medal issued (Kws. Taitien No.5306 and I.G.NO.177178). Commended for his praiseworthy action in saving life at sea during very bad weather conditions in Tolo Channel, Mirs Bay on the 23rd.Nov. 1939 (I.G.No.177075). Interned by Japanese during the Pacific War, released from Camp after the war and granted six months long leave from date of arrival at home port, overseas Pay issued by London Office from 18th Sep. 1945, the date of leaving China, to the date of returning to China.

* Dated from 26/7/46,the date of his arrival in Hongkong. 9/8/46 Reporting Reporting for duty at C.D. Office. 26/8/46 Detailed for duty on board CLT Wunhsing.

DATE.

Memo of Service in CMC

done officially, the doctor always made sure that a patient had made his Will.

A couple of hours after my father was admitted, the surgeon, accompanied by the hospital secretary, approached Leonard, who thought his time had come. To his surprise, he was informed that the Japanese were taking 150 'key men' out of the camp to an unknown destination, and that he was one of them. Because Leonard was in a great deal of pain, the surgeon asked if he could remain, but the reply was an emphatic 'no' and he was hauled out to get ready for the journey.

On 11th August 1945 after collecting what little personal items they could carry, my father amongst many others was herded onto a sampan at St Stephen's Beach and taken out to a small Japanese coaster, where they were pushed into the hold and battened down. After leaving the bay, Leonard could feel the swell on the beam and thought perhaps they were heading for Macau (a Portuguese colony 50 miles south of Hong Kong), on some exchange scheme. Later, he felt the swell aft, indicating that they were sailing up the East Lamma Channel. After an hour of extreme discomfort with temperatures at 34°C and humidity at over 90 per cent, they dropped anchor and the prisoners were allowed on deck for some air. It was then that Leonard discovered they were still in Hong Kong waters around Kowloon Bay.

The following morning everyone disembarked and marched several miles to a refugee camp at Ma Tau Chung which had been set up by Dr Selwyn Clarke to accommodate various neutral and foreign nationals who had not otherwise been rounded up. Contrary to Stanley, this was a properly prepared camp built to house Chinese refugees who had fled China for Hong Kong in 1938.

Leonard later learnt that the alleged 'key men' were from the indoor and coastal staff of the Chinese Maritime Customs, the Hong Kong Harbour Department, the Public

Works Department, Cable and Wireless, the Gas Company, the power companies and several others, and that they were to be taken to Canton to be executed. Not only did the Japanese want the men from these companies but their wives and children too, if there were any. For the next five days they were kept in the camp with no idea as to what was going on.

On 16th August 1945, the day after Japan had surrendered, someone outside the Ma Tau Chung Camp shouted that the war was over. The Japanese did nothing, so one of the inmates who spoke Urdu questioned an Indian guard, who confirmed that the surrender had indeed taken place. Later that day, American planes flew over the Colony dropping leaflets informing the prisoners that relief was on the way and that they should remain in the camps for the moment. There was a genuine concern that if internees were allowed out there could well be clashes between them and the Japanese and this had to be avoided at all costs.

At evening roll call, when the Japanese major took his usual position on a box, the prisoners refused to bow and began to laugh – this totally unnerved the major, who bolted to his quarters as fast as he could. The shoe was now on the other foot. Following this incident, the ex-POWs demanded proper food, only to be told there was none. As usual this proved to be a lie when a raid on the headquarters turned up hundreds of the stockpiled Red Cross parcels which the prisoners had never received. They were so emaciated and so hungry by now that there was a danger of overeating when they saw the food, so distribution had to be carefully handled.

At this point Gimson had the difficult task of taking charge of Hong Kong with no idea of when the British naval force could be detached from the British Pacific Fleet and head towards the Colony. Days went by, then two weeks later on

29th August 1945 an aircraft flew over Hong Kong dropping a message for the Japanese Commander from Admiral C.H.J. Harcourt. He instructed the Japanese to send an officer to the ship with details of where mines had been laid. Mr Makimura, the Japanese liaison officer, was reluctant to follow orders from Gimson and said he had no authority to negotiate with the British. Lieutenant General Tanaka, the senior officer commanding the area, was in Canton. Gimson informed Makimura that refusal to obey this order would be treated as a criminal offence, whereby Makimura radioed Harcourt informing him that he could not make arrangements for the surrender without Tanaka. Admiral Harcourt replied that he intended to enter Hong Kong the following day and Tanaka should be informed.

Commander D.H. Craven, the senior British naval POW, and Makimura flew out to HMS *Indomitable*, one of two aircraft-carriers (the other being HMS *Venerable*) accompanying Admiral Harcourt in *Swiftsure*, with detailed information of where the mines had been laid in the Hong Kong approaches. Craven informed Harcourt that no ships had passed in or out of Hong Kong for quite some time, strongly indicating that there could be mines in the area.

Another hazard that had been discovered was the wooden suicide boats lying up in Picnic Bay on Lamma Island. These boats were packed with explosives and manned with Japanese crews who would willingly die while destroying their targets. Several had already been discovered heading towards the Fleet, which British aircraft successfully destroyed, and the Fleet, with relieving naval forces, sailed into Hong Kong harbour. Food was quickly supplied to the various camps while preparation was made to release the POWs, who by now were getting extremely agitated. On 30th August Admiral Harcourt drove to Stanley Prison Camp for an emotional flag-raising ceremony which was attended by 2,000 internees.

*   *   *

In this relieving force was Margery's brother Tom on HMS *Duke of York* – Admiral Fraser's flagship of the British Pacific Fleet, which had just completed her voyage from Tokyo Bay in Japan, where the Japanese surrender was signed. Tom, after some difficulty and many enquiries (due to Leonard being moved from Stanley Camp on Hong Kong Island to Ma Tau Chung in Kowloon), located his brother-in-law, whom he had never met, and invited him on board for Sunday lunch, the day the surrender was signed in Hong Kong (31st August 1945).

In the wardroom Commander Tom Isaac tapped the bar hatch.

'May we have some drinks please?'

'Sorry sir,' said the marine, 'it's too early to open the bar.'

'My brother-in-law has been in a prison camp for three and a half years and has not had a drink in all that time,' retorted Tom.

'Oh that's different,' said the marine and promptly opened the hatch and poured a pint of ale. After one beer and one pink gin, Leonard, who prided himself on being able to consume much more than that, was almost on his back!

Not long after being released, my father was able to arrange for a passage to Australia on HMS *Vindex*, an escort carrier. My mother and I were on the wharf to meet him, but in spite of my excitement as a five-year-old, when the moment arrived shyness overcame all. The days that followed were difficult and it was to take some months before I understood that I now had a father.

On arrival Leonard was given a complete medical check-up, and apart from his gall bladder problem, bad malnutrition and some deterioration of his eyesight, he was declared reasonably fit considering everything.

After a couple of months' rest and good food at his parents' home in Adelaide it was time to pick up life again. Saying goodbye to his parents, whom we would not see again, we boarded a train for Sydney on Christmas Day 1945. The temperature was 45°C and the hot dry wind, so common at that time of the year, blew relentlessly.

Our passage was booked to the UK on a P & O liner, the SS *Mooltan*, a troopship which had formerly been used by the Australian mail service but was originally requisitioned as an armed merchant cruiser. In addition to being a troopship, she was also an RAPWI vessel (Repatriated Allied Prisoners of War and Internees) and infested with rats! Women and children were overcrowded in stuffy cabins, whilst the men were crowded below. One night while asleep, Margery felt something poking her toes. Thinking she had left some knitting needles at the bottom of the bunk, she moved her feet and thought no more about it. The next morning she discovered there were no needles – it had been a rat nibbling her toes. Another evening just as I was being put to bed, there was great excitement when a rat was seen running up and down the cabin – the men were called and my cricket bat, being the only useful weapon available, was used to dispose of the vermin; I was none too happy about that. Such were the conditions in the ship.

For some unknown reason the officer commanding the troops had an intense dislike for the civilians on board, perhaps because they were not subject to his discipline. He even stopped the cinema shows for those not in uniform. Between Fremantle and Colombo, Ceylon, he announced that a number of civilians were to be berthed down from the dormitories to hammocks in between decks, in order to accommodate a party of WRENS who were boarding in Colombo. Several civilians, including Leonard, approached the Captain about this, with the result that the WRENS did not embark and the civilians stayed where they were. This did not improve the relationship with the OC troops, who appeared to develop even more animosity towards the civilians.

On arrival at Southampton six to seven weeks later in the spring of 1946, the SS *Mooltan* was delayed by a drifting mine in the Spithead – a common sight after the war and a real danger to ships. This delayed disembarkation while the ship anchored off-shore for the night until the mine was cleared. Meanwhile, the OC Troops had posted dis-embarkation orders, putting POWs and internees last on the list. The following morning after berthing, the Mayor of Southampton stepped aboard to welcome the civilian passengers who were asked to disembark first – this must have been the final straw for the OC. From Southampton we journeyed by train to Ellesmere in Shropshire, where another of Margery's brothers was a bank manager and where she and I would stay for the next year.

Leonard was admitted to hospital in Oswestry, where he finally had his gall bladder removed. Because of his weak condition, the doctor advised that he should have an epidural instead of anaesthetic, which meant that he would be totally conscious throughout the operation. During this, the doctors talked to Leonard, discussing what they were doing or about to do and how it was all proceeding. They were amazed at his apparent stamina; it was the biggest stone they had ever come across. The day after he was discharged from the hospital, he felt so fit that he went to the races! No further problems were encountered during his lifetime; he was so proud of the size of the stone that he kept it in a jar for many years until my mother got fed up and threw it out; he was most upset!

Four months later, Leonard was informed that he should prepare to return to China. Because of the lack of accommodation in Hong Kong and uncertainty with the civil war in China, women and children were, as yet, unable to return, so once again the family was separated.

My father returned to Southampton, and boarded HMS *Ranee*, one of the many escort carriers heading to Hong Kong. Accommodation appeared to be allocated according to who you were. Hong Kong residents being repatriated whose passages were sponsored by the Colonial Office were accommodated in spare wardroom cabins, and those whose passages were paid for and sponsored by the Foreign Office were accommodated in spare petty officers' quarters. There was a wide variety of people down aft, ranging from the manager of the Bank Lines Hong Kong office to a group of Quakers, some Catholic priests and a few Chinese Maritime Customs staff. However, being in the aft end of the ship had its benefits – a tot of rum was distributed daily!

The passage would have been without incident had my father and two friends not missed the ship in Aden. Departure time had been posted as 1800 hours instead of 1700 hours, and just as they were boarding a launch at Steamer Point to return to the ship, they noticed HMS *Ranee* steaming away! They immediately reported to the port police, and it was suggested that they try to get a flight to Colombo and rejoin the ship there. They had no luck with that, but they did manage to board a ship which was bound for Penang.

Finally arriving in Penang, they still had to make their way to Singapore. With a few left-over traveller's cheques, they were able to hire a car and drive to Kuala Lumpur in Malaya, arriving at midnight. They had just enough money to hire another car and reached Singapore just before the banks closed for the weekend. Much to everyone's amazement they rejoined the ship at the naval base in Singapore and eventually sailed into Hong Kong waters. From there Leonard boarded a Dutch vessel to Shanghai, where he was, once again, commissioned into the Chinese Maritime Customs.

RESUMPTION OF CUSTOMS

Customs functions had to be resumed as soon as possible at all the occupied ports and the Inspectorate, which had already moved back to Shanghai from Chungking, re-opened on 1st January 1946. After 50 years of Japanese rule, the Custom Houses in Formosa (Taiwan) were once more under Chinese control and a reunited and experienced staff looked to the future with confidence.

By the end of the war, 90 per cent of their fleet had disappeared and of the few handed back by the Japanese, only one or two were seaworthy. Eight 'Admirable' Class minesweepers, eight YMS wooden minesweepers and three net-working vessels, all of which had been demilitarised, were purchased from the US Navy. The first 16 were to be used for preventive work and the net-working vessels for buoy laying and light tendering.

Leonard was appointed captain of CPS *Yuenhsing* (referred to as *A4*) in October 1946. With a crew of 80 and an armament of 6 very doubtful Japanese rifles, they sailed south to Hong Kong, where they were to be based.

One of his first assignments was to sail to Hainan Island, south of Hong Kong and Macau. It was in nature a 'snooping' trip to obtain information on some of the Customs pre-war vessels which had been formerly based in Hoihow and removed by the Japanese. First port of call was Chinhai (Qiong hai) on the north east coast of the island. An old pre-war survey had been made by the Customs but there was no way of knowing whether the chart was current, or whether changes had taken place over the years, and more importantly, whether the port was mined. For a while the crew watched the course taken by several heavily laden junks and decided that the deep water appeared to be as shown on the chart. *A4* then anchored just inside the entrance for the night.

The next morning Leonard went to visit the village elder, but was told by the Chief of Police that he was away on business. More than likely the elder was a smuggler and seeing the Customs arrive, decided to disappear smartly! In order to appear friendly and helpful, the Chief of Police suggested that Leonard might like to visit the Japanese dockyard and barracks, so with one of his midshipmen as interpreter and two armed guards, they set off on foot. Apparently unknown to anyone, the inhabitants had been told to make the foreigners welcome and in so doing released a barrage of firecrackers which nearly caused the patrol to throw themselves into the nearest ditch!

Further down the coast three caves were discovered which had been excavated by the Japanese to house their suicide motor boats. These wooden boats were about 15 feet long and fitted with an outboard engine. When in use they would carry a 4,000-lb charge secured to the stem head. In all, there were 24 boats in the cave but all engines and charges had been removed.

The next port of call was Yulin on the furthest southern tip of Hainan. This port had been developed by the Japanese as a naval base and used as an outlet for the iron mines a short distance north west of the port. The port itself was littered with sunken and half sunken wrecks as a result of the American bombing. Only one Customs vessel was found and that was well beyond repair.

Leonard and his crew spent Christmas 1946 in Yulin – not a particularly exciting place to be. They tied up alongside a

China merchant liberty ship anchored off the port, where he was able to swap 20 tons of fresh water for a bottle of gin. A swap which was appreciated on both sides.

Normal patrols for the Customs were 10 days out followed by four days in port. From Hong Kong the area covered was from North Formosa to Pakhoi on the Indo-China border. At this time a shortage of staff was quite a problem and in the first two years Leonard had no fewer than 12 officers in his ship. If the officers were good, they were soon put in command of small craft, if they were not, they did not remain in the service.

Although staff were reasonably well paid, many, unfortunately, fell victim to temptation, and corruption spread rapidly. Many of the older, more experienced hands, like my father, spent as much time watching their compatriots as they did catching smugglers.

Early one morning a small Customs fleet was anchored to the north west of Hong Kong, when Leonard noticed one of the launches leaving the patrol line, followed at intervals by three others. As the last one was leaving, my father ordered it to pull alongside *A4* and enquired as to where he was going. 'To base to have breakfast,' he was told. A strange answer since all the launches were equipped with cooking facilities. He was then ordered to get back on patrol and wait to be relieved. This was an obvious case where officers had been bribed to vacate a particular area at a particular time so that the smugglers could pass through. Often the officer of the watch would turn a blind eye to a suspicious craft rather than call the captain to the bridge.

One early morning as Leonard approached the bridge, he noticed a small motor coasting vessel known as a 'puff puff' steaming away towards the horizon with heavy black smoke belching from its stack.

'Why was I not called to the bridge?' said Leonard, annoyed after noticing the 'puff puff'.

'I thought it was just an ordinary trader,' answered the officer of the watch.

The 'puff puff' was chased and two of its crew members were taken on board *A4* as hostages, while their boat was towed to one of the Customs central stations. Suddenly there was a lot of shouting between some of the crew aft of *A4* and someone on the 'puff puff'. Asked where they were heading, the hostages said they had come from the Pescadores and were bound for Canton with a load of sugar.

After anchoring at Samun, a very indignant local informed Leonard that he was not one of the 'puff puff' crew, but had been engaged to pilot the boat into Hong Kong waters. On being asked how he was going to be paid he produced a piece of paper with the name and address of the consignee of the cargo in Hong Kong. The hostages then gave in and their craft was seized with the consigned sugar plus about 1½ hundredweight of melted down silver dollars, as well as four kerosene tins full of silver dollars.

In addition to not having very enthusiastic officers, Leonard was often given false information so that his ship would be 50 or more miles away from where the smuggling was to take place. It was difficult, at times, to know what to do.

As so often happens in certain services, corruption went right to the top, and when one very senior commissioner retired early because he had supposedly won, not one, but two very valuable sweepstakes, it was all very suspicious. Because of his complete integrity, Leonard became a nuisance to those who wanted to make a dishonest profit. He had just discovered that a large cache of gold and arms was to be smuggled in the area within a week, when he received a message which read: 'Return to Hong Kong immediately'. He knew why and submitted an extremely strong patrol report which resulted in his being asked to see a doctor. It was suggested that he take 28 days' 'sick' leave. Obviously the doctor had already been briefed.

CHINA – CIVIL WAR

When the atomic bomb was dropped on Hiroshima, Japan, on 6th August 1945 followed by another on Nagasaki three days later, Emperor Hirohito finally surrendered and the Pacific war came to an end.

But as one war ended another war was being re-ignited and the old feud between the Nationalists and Communists, who had only agreed to unite to rid China of the Japanese, was still festering. There was immediate rivalry for the areas occupied by the defeated Japanese.

The Communist forces could have taken the surrender of Nanking and Shanghai since they were situated close to both cities, but Chiang Kai-shek requested that the Americans airlift his troops into Shanghai and other former Japanese acquired territories, thus thwarting the Communists. Chiang, however, made a huge error in asking the Japanese military command to continue to administer Shanghai until he and the Americans arrived. The Japanese High Command had already left the city and the Japanese soldiers patrolled the streets; they loaded ships with goods they had confiscated from the Chinese; trucks full of booty were driven to their planes at Kiangwan airfield and the Kempei Tei (Secret Police) at the infamous Bridge House had plenty of time to burn all evidence that could have been used against them at the war trials.

The euphoria that accompanied the end of the Japanese war was soon to disappear as those who had welcomed the Nationalists began to turn against them, and the Government, with disgust.

Between VJ day and the end of 1948, the Americans had poured 3 billion dollars' worth of goods into China; medicines, food, clothing etc. supplied by international relief agencies were not reaching the intended recipients. Most of it could be seen on stalls around the city or being auctioned off, still with the Red Cross wrappings. Even blood plasma from the American Red Cross ended up on drugstore shelves.

Who was responsible for all this? Even before the misappropriation of relief funds to the black market, the same Kuomintang top officials led by the Chiangs, Soongs and Kungs had siphoned off large amounts of American funds into their own pockets. In fact, even during the Sino-Japanese War when a plane bound for Washington, DC, with supposedly secret documents, had to ditch because of fire, it was discovered to have been carrying US currency which the Soong family was sending to the US. It was never really revealed just how much Chiang's wife and his in-laws had stashed away in overseas bank accounts, but it was considered to be in the billions.

Behind so-called patriotism, Chiang Kai-shek and the Kuomintang proved to be hypocritical, selfish and incompetent of managing China's economy. Before the war, the Nationalists began issuing paper notes to cover the lack of gold reserves; by 1946 they had released 4.5 billion Chinese dollars. Inflation reached astonishing heights, making the notes worth less than the paper they were printed on. In 1948 the value of the American dollar to a Chinese dollar would have been more than 1 million. My father's salary was handed to him in a suitcase – bundles of dirty paper money tied with string and totally worthless in spite of the fact it was 5 million (Chinese) dollars!

There appears to be only one reason for the unprecedented inflation and that was because of Chiang's commitment to war against the Communists, for which he had budgeted 80 per cent of Government funds to his armed forces. It was this inflation which nearly brought Chiang's Government down even before the Communists. Chiang refused to share power with the Communists and was confident that he would succeed in removing the PLA (People's Liberation Army) from areas they had already captured. He did not reckon on the defectors from his army or that the Communists were gradually winning the loyalty of the Chinese people.

The Americans at this point were becoming increasingly worried by constant civil war in China. General George Marshall, a retired US Army Chief-of-Staff was sent as a mediator by President Truman and within one month had managed to secure a truce between the two sides which held up in most areas, except Manchuria. With the failure of the accord in February 1946, and the evacuation of the former Japanese puppet state of Manchukuo by the Soviets, fighting broke out once more.

The Soviets completed their evacuation of Manchuria by 3rd May 1946 and for the remainder of the year the Communists and Nationalists fought continuously for Manchuria, and the war raged on. During 1947 the Communists gradually consolidated their power, and feeling secure enough to mount an offensive, decided to attack the Liaosi corridor in September. One of the most strategic battles was fought over this corridor, held by the Nationalists.

Hong Kong in 1947 was still recovering from the trauma of the Japanese occupation. Collaboration by locals with the Japanese had been rife during the occupation and over 50 suspects were held to face committal proceedings on charges of treason. Others were charged under the Emergency Regulations with committing acts with intent to assist the enemy. This did not carry the death penalty but out of 30 people tried, 5 were hanged, 22 imprisoned for periods of up to 15 years, 2 sentenced to 1 day, 1 acquitted and 1 escaped.

RETURN TO HONG KONG

Finally, as authorities declared Hong Kong more secure, a trickle of wives and children began to return – a time my mother was so looking forward to. I was now six years old and had not known my birth-place or seen much of my father since he was repatriated, so for me it was an exciting adventure. We were to board the ship at Southampton towards the end of January 1947 but the roads were almost impassable with snow. Through friends of my uncle, we were loaded into a horse box with our trunks, and sitting on bales of straw headed towards Shrewsbury station. With its wheels wrapped in chains it was the only vehicle available and probably one of the few to be able to negotiate some of the steep roads that led to the station. Eventually arriving safely in Southampton, we set sail in SS *Strathmore* for Hong Kong.

I have many vivid memories of the voyage, not least the 'gullie gullie' men at Port Said and the local children who would dive off the ship for coins we threw into the sea. It was my first experience of being in a swimming pool, much to my mother's anguish. She would put me to bed each night while she went for dinner, but I had better things to do and the swimming pool called. In a pool with a depth of 8 feet and no shallow end, I would cling to the rail and pull myself round and round until I heard an angry voice say 'Get out of there at once!' No amount of threats could keep me from doing this – it was like honey to a bee. One day I just let go and paddled from corner to corner but all I got for my pride was a smacked bottom! Little did my mother know that it was just the start of a swimming career, of lessons, and hours of training at the YMCA pool in Salisbury Road, Kowloon.

We arrived at Kowloon Wharf, Hong Kong, six weeks later and my father met us at the dockside, when I had my first exciting ride in a rickshaw. I sat on my mother's lap in one and my father went in another.

It was not long before there was an incredible surge of growth in Hong Kong. Refugees from China, fleeing from the Communists, flooded in across the border and the Colony faced enormous problems as it tried to cope with the demand for housing, education and health care. Rebuilding did not get under way until 1948 and until then, pressure on accommodation led to the Hong Kong Government requisitioning empty property and local hotels, such as the famous Peninsula Hotel in Kowloon, where we were to live, and which was to become our playground for the next four years. The charge was HK$8.00 per person per day – today, a room would cost anything from HK$400 to HK$2,000 per day.

Recovery in road traffic was so rapid that a one-way street system had to be introduced into the Central area of Hong Kong Island, but driving was easy and many a Sunday, friends who had a car (we did not) would drive us all to the beach at Castle Peak or Tai Po in the New Territories.

CHINA'S FINAL CAMPAIGN

On 12th September 1948, after fierce counter-attacks by the Nationalists, the decisive moment in the Manchurian campaign arrived when they were defeated by the Communists. Chiang ordered his Manchurian garrisons to fall back and as the three Nationalist armies fought their way south, at least 300,000 troops were lost. By 1st November, Mukden had fallen into Communist hands and they were in complete control of Manchuria.

In late 1948, Leonard was ordered to go to Canton to pick up the Governor of Kwangtung Province, T.V. Soong, whom he had met on several occasions. Although Soong could have taken the normal river steamer he probably felt safer on a Customs ship, apart from the fact that it was the Government's way of showing how reliant it was on the Customs Service.

This was again demonstrated when the Inspector General was instructed to transfer the national gold reserves to Formosa (Taiwan). These transfers, which amounted to over 200 tons of gold and silver, were made in small Customs vessels manned by handpicked Nationalist officers, although the Government had large, well-armed, naval vessels available. Under cover of darkness, Nationalist troops cordoned off the Bund and gold and silver was removed by coolies carrying the parcels of gold bullion on bamboo poles from the vaults of the Bank of China, Shanghai. It was then loaded onto small boats along the Bund and ferried to larger vessels at anchor, which then sailed to Formosa. Chiang had been preparing the island as his stronghold for some time, not only shipping the Government's remaining equipment and troops, but most of its precious imperial treasures as well.

Following the fall of Manchuria, a huge campaign was launched – the Battle of the Huai Hai was fought along the Lunghai railway line and would last until January 1949. On 21st January 1949, Chiang Kai-shek resigned as President of Nationalist China, General Fu Tso-yi surrendered the Nationalist garrison in Peking and Mao Tse-tung moved his capital from Yunan to Peking. The Nationalists were defeated.

Chiang Kai-shek, realising that it was over, had only one option – withdraw to the offshore islands where they would be safe from the Communists, who had virtually no navy. Troops were evacuated to Quemoy off Amoy, Matsu off Foochow, and Matsu off Wenchow, and Chiang left for Formosa, where he was to preside for the next 26 years. In his annual birthday speech he would announce that the Nationalists were preparing for an invasion of China, but for Chiang it was but a pipe dream. He died in 1975.

* * *

In 1949, Mr Lester Little, who was by now the new Inspector General of the Chinese Maritime Customs (having been appointed in 1943 following Mr Joly's retirement) received orders from the Minister of Finance to select some Chinese Customs staff to accompany him to Canton and then to Taiwan to set up a Customs administration. My father was one of the remaining staff to go in his old ship *A4*, and after three months in Taikoo, all Customs officers were paid off. They were informed that they would receive a pension, but this never materialised and many officers, like my father, at the age of 40 years and over, had to find alternative work and start again. Even compensation for being in a Japanese camp was withheld and eventually given to the Hong Kong University.

This was the sad ending of nearly 100 years of the Chinese Maritime Customs, a service my father loved, and one best described in the words of Sir Robert Hart (Inspector General 1863) to Lord Salisbury in 1885:

> The Service which I direct is called the Chinese Customs Service, but its scope is wide and its aim is to do good work for China in every possible direction.

Throughout its long history this was the directive that guided all members of the service and one of which they were so proud.

BIBLIOGRAPHY

Barber, Noel, *The Fall of Shanghai* (Coward. McCann & Geoghegan, New York, 1979).

Birch, Alan & Cole, Martin, *Captive Years: The Occupation of Hong Kong 1941–45* (Heinemann Asia, 1982).

Carew, Tim, *The Fall of Hong Kong* (Anthony Blond Ltd, 1960).

Dong, Stella, *Shanghai* (Harper Collins).

Gittins, Jean, *Stanley Behind Barbed Wire* (Hong Kong University Press, 1982).

Hall, B. Foster, *The Chinese Maritime Customs: An International Service 1854–1950* (Trustees of the National Maritime Museum, 1977).

Roland, Charles G., *Long Night's Journey into Day* (Wilfrid Laurier University Press, 2001).

GLOSSARY

Coolie	manual labourer
Godown	warehouse (from Malay *gadang*)
Junk	large wooden sailing vessel
Rickshaw	two-wheeled carriage pulled by a man
Sampan	small wooden boat
Tai tai	Chinese word for wife
Tiffin	lunch